Alumni Association

Quarter Centennial Anniversary Souvenir

Of the Southern Illinois State Normal University

Alumni Association

Quarter Centennial Anniversary Souvenir
Of the Southern Illinois State Normal University

ISBN/EAN: 9783337007621

Printed in Europe, USA, Canada, Australia, Japan

Cover: Foto ©ninafisch / pixelio.de

More available books at **www.hansebooks.com**

Quarter Centennial

ANNIVERSARY SOUVENIR

OF THE

Southern Illinois State Normal University.

---◆---

PUBLISHED BY THE

ALUMNI ASSOCIATION.

---◆---

CARBONDALE FREE PRESS,

1899.

To the Memory of Dr. Robert Allyn,

Who, for eighteen years was President of the Southern Illinois State Normal University, and whose noble life and untiring labors so largely established the character of our school and left so lasting an impress upon its students,

We, the Alumni, Dedicate this Volume.

We honored and revered him in life; we mingled our tears at his death; and as the years go by the sacredness in which his memory is held shall ever increase.

Contents.

The S. I. N. U. from its Founding to the Fire.   5
    Dr. D. B. Parkinson.

Burning of the Normal......................   17
    Rev. F. M. Alexander.

The Fire of '83............................   20
    Prof. Jas. H. Brownlee.

Elegy on the Old Southern Normal..........   26
    Mrs. Carrie L. Mount.

History of S. I. N. U. Since 1883...........   29
    Miss Martha Buck.

Our Trustees—Past and Present............   40
    Prof. Geo. H. French.

The Influence of the S. I. S. N. U...........   48
    Prof. H. W. Shryock.

Our Presidents—

Robert Allyn, LL. D...*Mrs. C. W. Parkinson*   54
John Hull, A. M.......*Dr. C. M. Galbraith*   63
H.W. Everest, A.M., LL.D.*Prof. G. W. Smith*   66
D. B. Parkinson, Ph. D...*Miss Helen Bryden*   70

Zetetic Literary Society....................   75
    Miss Mary Buchanan.

10. Socratic Literary Society.................. 81
     Hon. W. H. Warder.

11.. Life's Awakening (anniversary poem)....... 87
     Rev. F. M. Alexander.

12. Our Alumni Dead........................ 90
     Miss Mary Wright.

13. Twenty-Fifth Anniversary (proceedings)..... 99
     Prof. G. H. French.

14. Faculty—Past and Present—
     Past.. *Dr. Parkinson, Prof. Alvis, Miss Buck* 148
     Military Department....*Dr. D. B. Parkinson* 157
     Present................*Prof. C. E. Allen* 158

15. Sketches of Alumni (compiled)............ 165

Preface.

The Alumni Association at their last annual meeting, June 16, 1898, discussed several propositions, which, when once put in operation, will materially effect the future history of the S. I. N. U. The three propositions of most importance were: That provisions be made for a permanent summer term. Second, that at least one member of the Board of Trustees shall be an alumnus. Third, that we publish a souvenir volumn setting forth the sailent features in the history of the school.

The Faculty and Board of Trustees promptly took up the summer term proposition, and a successful beginning was made in the same summer of '98, and the prospects for '99 give evidence of the demand for its permanent establishment. Owing, however, to the lack of the General Assembly to supply the necessary funds for this purpose the future of the summer term is somewhat problematical.

No united effort has yet been made to secure representation on the Board of Trustees, and perhaps nothing can be done until our wishes are more earnestly and unitedly urged upon those who have the appointing power.

It is the regret of the Publication Committee that the advice and suggestions from a greater number of the Association could not be obtained in our efforts to carry out the third wish of the Alumni. Many perplexing questions might have been easily disposed of which have caused delay and hesitation. Such questions as what shall be the essential features of the book, and how shall the expenses of the book be met? Compelled, under the circumstances, to act without the council of all the members we have made an earnest effort to select such material as will be of permanent interest, both to the Association and the school.

Perhaps, at no other time in the history of the school has there been a more urgent need for a complete record of all the early facts connected with the founding, early struggles and growth of this institution. In the lapse of a quarter of a century many of the original actors who have hitherto supplied the early historic facts have passed away, and in a few years all data from eye witnesses will be unattainable. For this reason much space has been given to the historic phase, and especially, that it shall be written by those whose lives are a part of what they write. Another object of the Committee is to answer the insinuation: "Can any good thing come out of Egypt?" More than once has Southern Illinois by the genius of her sons and the excellence of her institutions refuted the charge, but there are still those living within our own commonwealth who look upon Egypt as a land without railroads, destitute of an educational spirit, and withal a fertile field for missionary labor. To answer, once for all, the educational part of the criticism, candid facts pertaining to the "Influence of the Southern Normal in Egypt," will effectually set this question at rest.

Believing that there is a stronger desire to-day, among the Alumni, to make Southern Illinois a greater factor in the educational councils of the State, to which this Normal University shall contribute her full share, we send forth this volumn, hoping it will prove of permanent interest to the Association, and that it will find a responsive chord in the heart of every true friend of education.

FIRST BUILDING.

The Southern Illinois Normal University From Its Founding to the Fire.

THE founding of an educational institution marks an epoch in any community, and often affects the commonwealth in no small degree. It indicates a progressive spirit and a realization of the most vital interest of any people. Our forefathers were not ignorant of, nor indifferent to, these paramount values to a State and Nation. They made prompt provision for a liberal education among their youth, a condition which has had a decided influence in shaping the type and character of our people. The establishment and prosperous career of Harvard and Yale Universities made it possible to create and equip like educational centers throughout our land during the generations which followed. Liberal-minded men and generous legislators have contributed freely toward this agency of genuine culture, and placed our citizenship in a position to meet the grave problems of an advancing civilization. One of the most marked products of this effort is the public school system now so generally installed in this imperial nation of ours.

The evolution of the educational problem soon developed the need of the special training of teachers for their specific duties. Normal schools were soon brought into existence to meet this demand. Less than forty years after the "Prairie State" was admitted into the Union her General Assembly passed an act establishing her first Normal School. About ten years later, by the same authority, the second school of this character was provided for.

Four years ago the State authorized the erection and equipment of two additional schools for the training of her teachers. During the last session of the legislature a fifth school was brought into existence. From the above account it is evident that Illinois has been ready to respond to the demand for skilled workmen in her schoolrooms. The State that boasts of Lincoln, Grant, and Logan may well feel proud of her Normal Schools.

The second in the above list, and the subject of this sketch, is closely coupled with the advanced steps taken in educational matters in the progressive west. The bill creating this institution was passed by the General Assembly of 1869, and received the signature of Governor John M. Palmer April 20. In due time the Charter Trustees, as they were called, were selected, viz: Capt. David Hurd, of Cairo; Gen. Eli Boyer, of Olney; Col. Thos. M. Harris, of Shelbyville; Rev. Elihu J. Palmer, of Belleville, and Samuel J. Flanagan, of Benton.

After a long delay and much discussion the site for the new Normal School was determined upon. Much to the disappointment of Du Quoin, Centralia, Carlyle and a few other rival towns, Carbondale was the fortunate winner of the prize. The Board selected a tract of ground about three-quarters of a mile south of the Illinois Central station immediately adjacent to the right of way of the railroad on the west side. The tract of land, consisting of twenty acres, had recently been a strawberry field.

Ground was soon broken and the work begun. The corner-stone was laid with impressive ceremonies by the Masonic fraternity on May 17, 1870.

The contract had been let to Mr. J. M. Campbell, one

of Carbondale's most active and most progressive citizens, for the sum of $225,000.

During the erection of the building, and while superintending the work, Mr. Gampbell was killed by the falling of a large timber. This sad accident delayed the work for some time, and finally a Building Commission was appointed to complete the structure, consisting of John Wood, of Cairo, Elihu J. Palmer, of Carbondale; Hiram Walker, of Jonesboro; R. H. Sturgiss, of Vandalia; Nathan Bishop, of Marion, and F. M. Malone, of Anna.

By this change in the management of the erection of the building the final cost exceeded that named in the original contract. The entire cost was placed at $265,000.

The architecture was of the Norman style, with trimmings of sand-stone in two colors. Its extreme length was 215 feet; extreme width 109 feet. It had a basement of 14 feet in the clear; two stories, one 18 feet, the other 22 feet, and a Mansard story of 19 feet. The basement was devoted to the heating apparatus, laboratory, work-room for the carpenter. and residence for the janitor; the Mansard to lecture hall, library, museum and literary society rooms; the main two stories to offices, study hall and recitation rooms.

Upon the completion of the building Governor Beveridge appointed the following gentlemen to serve as Trustees, whose first duty was to select a Faculty of Instruction and furnish the several departments with suitable furniture and apparatus: Thos. S. Ridgeway, Shawneetown; James Robarts, M. D., Carbondale; Edwin S. Russell, Mt. Carmel; Lewis M. Phillips, Nashville; Judge Jacob W. Wilkin, Marshall. The Board was organized as follows: President, Mr. Ridgeway; Secretary, Dr. Robarts; Treasurer, John G. Campbell; Registrar, Charles W. Jerome. Mr. Ridgeway remained the President of the Board for the first eighteen years, when his term expired, and the newly-elected Governor appointed an entirely new Board. He was reappointed by Governor Tanner, but failing health caused him to decline the honor. A few months subsequent to his non-acceptance he was removed from the scenes of this life much beloved by a large circle of friends socially, financially and politically.

The Board of Trustees gave much of their time and thought to the establishment of the school on a broad and substantial basis. In the early part of '74 they elected the following persons to constitute the Faculty of Instruction, named in the order as published in the first Catalogue:

Robert Allyn, Principal, Mental Science Ethics and Pedagogics.

Cyrus Thomas, Natural History and Physiology.

Charles W. Jerome, Registrar, Languages and Literature.

Enoch A. Gastman, (elect), Mathematics.

Daniel B. Parkinson, Natural Philosophy and Chemistry.

James H. Brownlee, Reading, Elocution and Phonics.

Granville F. Foster, History and Geography.

Alden C. Hillman, Princicipal of High School; teacher in Normal Department.

Martha Buck, Grammar and Etymology.

VOCAL MUSIC.

Drawing and Calisthenics—Julia F. Mason, Principal of Primary and Model School.

Hon. A. D. Duff (elect), Dean of Law Department.

Miss Mason was not elected till September, after the school had opened on the 6th of said month. Mr. Gastman, after one year's consideration of the matter, declined to accept the position offered him, his choice of work having been previously offered to Dr. Thomas. His place was filled by the election of Prof. John Hull in the autumn. Miss Buck and the writer of this early sketch have remained as members of the Faculty from the first. Prof. Brownlee was called to the chair of Rhetoric and Oratory in the University of Illinois in '86. In '97 he returned to the Faculty of the Southern Normal,

The writer was elected Secretary of the Faculty on July 6, '74. and continued to serve in that capacity till September, '92, when, because of being made Registrar at the June meeting of the Board, he resigned in favor of Prof. S. M. Inglis, who was succeeded by Prof. George W. Smith in September. '94, who is still serving in that capacity.

Returning to the further history of the building: It was completed June 30. '74, and dedicated with ceremonies commensurate with the importance of the occasion the following day, July 1. These dedicatory exercises were of great significance to the cause of education in Southern Illinois, the entire state, and, in fact, in the middle west. They gave promise of a new era in school matters in these regions. The program of the day was a well-selected one; the best talent was secured, and the vast concourse of people assembled on that memorable day retired from the scene with renewed zeal, greater courage and a deeper conviction of duty pertaining to educational interests. The speakers were as follows: Dr. Richard Edwards, President Illinois State Normal University; Dr. Charles H. Fowler, President Northwestern University; Dr. Robert Allyn, the newly-elected President of the new school, Hon. J. J. Bird, Cairo; and Hon. Thos. Ridgeway, President, Board of Trustees. Hon. Newton Bateman, then State Superintendent, was to have given the principal address, but on account of sickness could not be present. His place was ably filled by Doctor Edwards.

The work of the institution was inaugurated by the opening of a special session on the day after dedication. This session continued six weeks. The first regular session opened September 6, and closed June 17, '75, with an enrollment of 396. Number of pupil teachers first year, 26.

Soon after the opening of the school a demand for a literary society was so manifest that in the early part of the term a society for this purpose was organized. A suitable name with which to christen this new-born child of the young mother was a matter of deep concern. After much counsel and searching for a name those in charge of the matter decided on the rare but significant title of "Zetetic," which means "A Seeker," a name employed by some of the Pyrrhonists. This society has done much to establish and maintain a high ideal in genuine culture; it has been a potent factor to encourage and foster an elevated literary taste. Its motto, "Learn to Labor and to Wait," has inspired hundreds of young people to act nobly along these two lines of true endeavor. The opportunities of a single society soon proved inadequate for the demand. On October 1, '75, a petition was granted for the organization of a "Debating Club." On the evening of October 15 the Constitution and By-laws were indorsed by the Faculty. This organization was at first exclusive in its character, no ladies being admitted. However, this peculiar condition could not long endure the pressure from without, neither could it cope with the older organizations in enlarging its membership. Its name was changed to the Socratic Literary Society, and in due time the young ladies were admitted to its fold. The spirit of the society has ever been in harmony with that of the noted character whose name it bears. Its motto, "*Nulla Vera, Felicitas Sine Sapientia*" ("no true happiness without knowledge"), has implanted in the breasts of a multitude of ambitious youth the secret of true success.

A few years later (1880) the members of the special session organized themselves for literary work and gave to their society the name of "The Allyn Literary Society."

The Zetetic Society was given the northwest room in the Mansard story, and the Socratic Society the southwest room on same floor. The Library occupied the northeast room, and the Museum the southeast room. The lecture-room was on the same floor, in the middle of the building, immediately over the Normal or Assembly Hall, which was on the third floor.

The year '77-'78 opened up with a new departure, quite unusual in normal schools. A military officer had been detailed by the War Department of the Government to take charge of a military department in the Southern Illinois Normal. Captain Thos. J. Spencer has the honor of organizing this new branch of instruction in the new normal school of Illinois. The equipment for this new line of work, such as bayonets, rifles, cannons, caissons, etc., were soon on the ground and ready for use. This department was discontinued at the close of the school year of '91.

Aside from the regular duties of the school there were in the early years occasions of special interest that are interwoven in its history. Among these that of tree-planting day ranks as one of the most pleasant, not only for the immediate pleasure connected therewith, but for the permanent benefits which have followed. This practice of the school was instituted many years before "Arbor Day" was established in the State. On these gala-days the young men went into the woods near by and procured suitable trees and shrubs and planted them in the campus of the University, while the young ladies prepared a bountiful dinner, which was served in the lower corridor with all the elaborateness of a banquet.

Much of the beauty of the grounds to-day is due to these early efforts of faculty and students. The group of large maple trees in the north central part of the grounds in the shape of an "R" was planted by the representatives of Randolph county; the large group of thirty-five maple trees in the southwest portion of the campus was planted by the thirty-five members of an arithmetic class under Prof. Hillman; and a beautiful star of evergreen trees was planted just to the east of the north gate. But this last and many others were removed by changing the grade of the ground about the building several years later. Had the first trees and the many vines which Dr. Allyn planted been allowed to remain, the grounds would have an older look and a large part of the present building would now be covered, as is a portion of the north and the south ends. In fact, the building would resemble the older residences of Washington, D. C.

The biennial visit from the legislative committees was another event of deep interest. The dignity of the guests and the issue at stake contributed to make the occasion one of much import to the school. In those days a larger delegation was sent to ascertain the needs of the State institutions than in recent years; and possibly with no better results. At that time the normal school problem was farther from solution than now and it required more care and watchfulness to secure an appropriation than at the present time.

On all such occasions Prof. Brownlee was ready with his elocutionary gifts to please and entertain the guests of the institution. He did his best on the occasion of the first visit from the Legislature, when the members were feasted in the southwest room now occupied by rooms 2 and 3 in the present building.

Commencement week, consisting of the Baccalaureate Sermon, Society Annual Entertainments, Class Day Exercises, Alumni Reunion and Banquet, and the climax of the whole, Graduating Exercises on Commencement Day with the general reception at night was the most important of the year. These annual gatherings have served to cement the various classes with the outgoing class into a closer friendship and allegiance to the institution, and to furnish the school an opportunity to exhibit the work of the students, and to hear an able address by some noted orator. No other such literary treat could be offered the people of the region represented by the school. Possibly no class of persons more heartily enjoyed these events than the former students, even though they had not completed a course of study.

The preparation of matter for the Centennial Exposition in the year of '75-'76 was an eventful task. The beautiful bronze medal and the artistic diploma which hangs in the Library as a companion piece of art to the one of similar character received from the Columbian Exposition bear evidence of the progressive spirit of the Faculty and students of the Southern Illinois Normal through the decades of the first quarter of a century of its history. The first action of the faculty looking toward an exhibition at the Centennial was taken on February 4, 1875.

The school sent material to the Paris Exposition as well as to those of our own country. This was decided upon March 27, 1878. The material was placed in the hands of John D. Philbrick.

Decoration Day has always been observed by the school. On many occasions the entire membership marched in a body to the center of the town, headed by the military band, followed by the cadets in uniform. Their military salute gave evidence of superior training in tactics. The first death in the family of a member of the Faculty was the demise of the wife of the writer, who had been a member of the first Faculty. She passed away on August 6, '79. On October 20, the same year, the wife of the President, a cultured and refined lady, was taken from the scenes of earth. In the summer of '82 Mrs. Prof. Hull was called to her reward after a lingering illness of several years.

On January 10, '83, the youngest daughter of Dr. Allyn, Miss Hattie, an accomplished young lady, was called to join her mother in the life beyond.

The first death in the Board of Trustees was that of Hon. L. M. Phillips in December, 1880, an account of which is noted elsewhere in this volume.

The model school, which was partially organized at the opening of the institution, was discontinued, as such, at the close of the first term of '76–'77. On September 11, '82, the Training Department was placed on a better basis, with Prof. Hull as Superintendent, and Miss Mary Sowers as Assistant. Since that time this department has been a very important factor in the institution, growing in popular favor and in efficiency.

In order to secure the highest degree of benefit from the regular meetings of the Faculty, different members volunteered to prepare papers bearing more or less on school subjects. One set of these papers is given below in the order of their presentation. The practice, however, was continued for some years. Dr. Allyn read the first paper on February 6, '80, on "What Constitutes a Good Teacher;" Prof. Jerome on "School Discipline;" Prof. Hull, "The Question and Its Answer;" the writer, on "Examinations;" Prof. Foster, on "How and What the Teacher Should Read;" Prof. Brownlee, on "Pronunciation;" Prof. Hillman, on "We and Us;" Miss Buck, on "Language Lessons;" Prof. French, on the "Principal's Report;" Miss Finley, on "The Relation of the Teacher to the Pupil." The above papers were prepared with great care and elicited much discussion, and they were indeed very helpful.

The institution has been characterized from its beginning by the most friendly feeling between teachers and students, Criticisms may have been justly made here and there as to its management, but the policy of placing the individual student upon his honor, and exercising a large measure of sympathy for the struggling young man or woman has resulted in a generation of more liberal minded, generous-hearted, and self-respecting citizens than would have been produced had a more rigid, narrow and exacting policy been adopted.

The writer's associates in the early Faculty will pardon any lack of special reference to the individual members, save the bare statement of the department in which they labored, which has been noted. I will be allowed,

I am sure, a few lines in which to refer to the President. Dr. Allyn brought to the new school, as its head, a strong personality, a large experience in educational matters, a cultured mind and a warm heart. This personality left a lasting impression for good upon the character of the school, the students and the Faculty which the Doctor gathered around him. However, an account of his life and work appears elsewhere, and the writer must refrain from further reference.

The various agencies set at work by the Board of Trustees accomplished great results; the school prospered and grew in general favor throughout the land and was justly regarded as the educational light of the southern part of Illinois. Many families from adjoining towns decided to make Carbondale their home because of its educational facilities. The eyes of the people were turned toward the Southern Illinois Normal University. But it was so ordered that the life of the school was not to be all sunshine. On the afternoon of November 26, 1883, a terrible calamity befell it. About two o'clock this noble edifice was discovered to be on fire. In a few hours it was a heap of ruins. The description of this catastrophe and the remainder of the history are portrayed by more fluent and gifted pens than the one which has narrated the events of the institution from the "founding to the fire."

Burning of the Normal.

F. M. ALEXANDER, CLASS OF '83.

On that quiet little village dawned the blessed Sabbath morn;
And a sense of peace and safety with the holy day was born.
Soon the chiming bells' sweet music, trembling on the morning air,
Called the happy, grateful people to the sacred house of prayer.
Labor's busy hands were folded, and no earthly cares annoyed,
While they praised the Great Good Giver, for the blessings they
    enjoyed:—
Grateful for the precious lessons they had studied in His Word;
Grateful for the love and mercy in the Gospel that they heard;
Thankful for domestic comforts and abundance that prevailed,
For their happy homes and firesides by no threatening foes assailed.
Best of all, they held that noble Fount of Learning, Light and Truth—
Source of knowledge, strength, and wisdom for the character of youth.
'Twas the pride of all the country and the glory of the town.

Now the day was fast approaching when the nation would express
Unto God her praise and gratitude for peace and happiness;
And fair Carbondale was waiting with all readiness to raise
Every heart and voice to Heaven in a choral hymn of praise;
For the generous Heaven above them sent on all its gentle rain,
And the grateful earth responded with her wealth of golden grain.

Thus with pleasure and abundance did the fleeting days glide on
Until Autumn's glories faded and her russet train was gone.
To and fro each morn and evening passed an earnest, faithful line
Of devoted students paying homage true at Learning's shrine.
Now the Sabbath day had ended and the morning bright and clear
Rose once more upon the village full of happiness and cheer.
In the people's hearts no warning, and no portent in the sky
Told them of the dire disaster and the danger lurking nigh.
Earnest students, faithful teachers, in each dear, familiar place,

Fell into the line of duty with their wonted zeal and grace.
But none dreamed that bright, glad morning, as they sought the noble
    Hall,
Ere that sad, sad day was ended they would see its proud dome fall.
No one knew, as they departed from the dear old class-room door,
That their class-mates would assemble in those places nevermore.
While those glad young minds were weaving Hope's bright fancies
    into woof,
Even then the fell destroyer was concealed beneath the roof,—
There in stealthy silence working with relentless, deadly hate,
Till his mastery was certain and resistance all too late.
But, as evil coming near us gives a warning sense of dread.
Soon the deamon was discovered in the timbers overhead.
Dumb with terror came the students down the massive brazen stair,
Through the doomed majestic portal, from the thick and stifling air,
Headed by their noble teachers—leaders faithful, tried and true,
Each brave heart sprang quickly forward and found noble work to do,
Pausing not to think of danger, plunging through the blinding smoke,
Rescuing their sacred treasures while the flames around them broke.
First in every place of duty in the seething, fiery storm,
Leading, planning, and directing, moved the tall and noble form
Of the aged Chief and Father, dauntless in the battle's brunt,
Until forced by loving followers from the thickening danger's front.
Honor, too, those noble women—maidens young and frail, and fair,
Vying with their sturdy brothers in heroic actions there.
Not one failed or faltered, but like heroes brave and true,
Lingered at the post of duty till there was no more to do.
Though the battle-ground was bloodless, with no clash of spear or
    shield,
Yet no brighter deeds of valor ever shown upon the field.

Far and near the sad entreaty had been flashing o'er the wire,
"For the love of Heaven, save us from the demon of the fire."
Prompt and manly was the answer, but assistance came too late,
And at last the noble structure was abandoned to its fate.
See! the mighty Foe, exulting, leaps upon the highest tower,
With his red eyes fiercly gleaming as he rages in his power,
Marking everything he touches with the burning seal of death,
While the very air is hissing with the fatal, fiery breath.

Hark! upon the ear anon breaks in the heavy, jarring sound
Of the massive granite falling from the turrets to the ground.
Pitying angels saw and wept and turned the winds against the fire;
But no power in earth or Heaven could now quench the demon's ire.
Hope now died in every bosom, bitter tears filled every eye,
As the cruel flames triumphant leaped exulting to the sky.
E'en the sun went down in sorrow, and the darkness of the night
Was lit up o'er all the country with the awful lurid light.

Mourn, oh broad and noble Prairie State—thy fair young daughter mourn;
Lift thy voice in lamentation for her body bruised and torn;
Mourn thy best and strongest safeguard from rebellion and from crime;
Mourn the loss thy children suffer—the best heritage of time.
We, thy children, in our bosoms are with deepest sorrow thrilled,
For we feel a place is vacant that can ne'er for us be filled.
O'er thy smouldering, blackened ruins other walls may rise as grand;
Other structures more imposing and with greater genius planned;
But the dear familiar objects we have cherished as our own
In their old accustomed places will no more by us be known.
All the hallowed rooms and places where we met in days of yore,
With their tender, sacred memories, time and wealth can ne'er restore.
We may find our books and pictures in some other fitting place;
We may meet again our teachers and each oft-remembered face;
But as many a child is saddened coming back to parents true,
Finding they have left the old home and are living in the new,
So when we return and find no more the things we've loved and known,
Each face will have a strange appearance and each voice a colder tone.

But the brightest stars are never seen till darkness veils the skies;
So we now see Hope's bright heralds from the gloom around us rise.
Round our Normal's broken standard friends will rally firm and brave,
While the voice of hate and envy will be buried in one grave.
Courage then! Stand by your colors, and with purpose true and strong
Move right onward with the leaders who have guided you so long;
And although our noble buildings in majestic ruins lie,
Yet the spirit they awakened in our hearts shall never die.

The Fire of '83.

MONDAY, November 26, 1883, was the saddest day in the history of the Southern Illinois Normal. On the afternoon of that day the first building was destroyed by fire. It was a massive and beautiful edifice that had cost the State two hundred and eighty-three thousand dollars. For nine years it had been the stately home of the young and growing school, and teachers and students were justly proud of it. Indeed, it was the pride and ornament of Southern Illinois, and its destruction threw a gloom over many hearts.

The origin of the fire was never certainly known. Nor need this concern us now. The flames did their cruel work thoroughly, whether, as some thought, they originated from spontaneous combustion, or whether, as others believed, they originated in an accident to the janitor's lantern.

The fire was discovered in the northwest corner of the Mansard roof at 20 minutes past 3 o'clock. Some of the four hundred students were busy with their books in the study hall, but a majority were in their classes in the various recitation rooms. Messengers were instantly sent to each room to make the appalling announcement: "The Normal is on fire!" Any fears that a panic might result proved groundless. Class after class was dismissed at once by the pale-faced teachers, who briefly instructed the pupils to go quickly to the hall and the corridors for books, hats, wraps, etc., and then leave the building.

When first seen by the janitor the fire was in the

attic just over the museum in the southeast corner. As soon as books and wraps had been deposited in a place of safety outside, a band of brave young men rallied around the president, Dr. Allyn, and other members of the faculty and rushed to the point of danger, the museum, in order to save the building, if possible. But to do this was soon found to be impossible. When the large hose connected with the tanks in the attic was trained upon the now flaming roof it was discovered that, owing to the height of the fire, only a feeble, ineffectual stream could be obtained. The flames gathered strength rapidly, and soon it became evident to the most hopeful that the building was doomed. Still, with inadequate weapons they fought on until the falling plaster, the bursting glass of the cases, the smoke and intense heat, warned them to leave.

Descending to the floor below, they informed the crowd of students and citizens that the building could not be saved—that all that could be done was to save as much of the furniture and library as possible. Fortunately the wind, which blew from the northwest, retarded in some measure the progress of the flames, so that there was time to act.

And now followed a scene of unselfish, heroic labor. Faculty, students, and citizens, all went energetically to work to save the furniture, musical instruments, and books. For two hours the work went on. No one who saw the sight will ever forget it. Pianos and organs were quickly lifted to sturdy shoulders and carried down the broad stairways and to safety as if the force of gravity had lost its pull. One piano only was lost—that belonging to the Socratic Literary Society, whose hall was just across the corridor from the museum. As there was no time to unscrew desks from the floor, they were torn from their fastenings by arms that seemed to have muscles of corded steel. The library was on the fourth floor in the northeast corner. It contained eight thousand volumes. Dr. Allyn was there to superintend the removal of his beloved books. Up and down the stairways went the hurrying, endless lines of students, those descending each bearing a huge armful of precious literature. Nor were men the only carriers. The young women were as brave, as active, and as helpful as the young men. Many of them were weeping silently in their excitement and grief, but still they went on carrying to safety great armfuls of books. Their faces were so grimed with smoke and perspiration that they were almost unrecognizable.

When I think of that unselfish band of students, and remember that at the risk of their young lives they bore to safety out of that roaring furnace of crackling flames and falling timbers property valued at twenty-five thousand dollars, and that they did this willingly and cheerfully for the school they so much loved, a lump rises in my throat and I feel like saying, "God bless them, every one!"

And now thoughtful observers of the progress of the flames saw that any further efforts would result in loss of life. So men were sent into the building to warn all to leave at once. Not a few were loth to quit, while in several instances it was necessary to use force in order to get the enthusiastic workers to a place of safety. There were several narrow escapes, but Providence so ordered it that not a life was lost, and for this we were all profoundly grateful.

The shadows of evening were now gathering and the tired host of smoke-stained teachers, students and citizens lingered at a safe distance to gaze upon a spectacle that was at once sorrowful and fascinating. How fiercely the flames leaped upward, as if glorying in the ruin they had wrought! How they seemed to riot in the unholy work! As I walked townward, about seven o'clock on that fateful evening, I remember that I often paused to look back upon the sublime but sorrowful spectacle presented by the ruins of the burning Normal. I remember, too, that they reminded me of the magnificent description of the burning castle in Scott's "Rokeby:"

> "In gloomy arch above them spread
> The clouded heaven lowered bloody red.
> Soon all beneath, through gallery long,
> And pendant arch, the fire flashed strong,
> Till from each loophole flashing l'ght,
> A spout of fire shines ruddy bright
> And, gathering to united glare,
> Streams high into the midnight air."

The normal building only had been burned; the school still lived stronger than before in the loyalty of professors and students and friends. That very evening a mass meeting was held in the Opera House. The citizens of Carbondale proved that no mistake had been made when the normal was located in their city. The authorities of the school were requested to go ahead with its daily work, and were informed that any rooms needed for their purpose in the business portion of the town were at their command; that if any rooms wanted for recitations were occupied, these would be immediately vacated. The generous proffer was appreciated, a committee appointed to select the most eligible rooms on the west side of the public square, and arrangements made to continue the work of instruction.

The next morning teachers and students gathered in one of the churches to confer regarding their duty in the presence of the appalling calamity. The effects of the excitement and exertions of the preceding day were visible in the pale, drawn faces of all. The importance of events and actions is measured by their results. Thus measured, that meeting was the most important in an educational point of view of any ever held in Southern Illinois. Speeches were made both by teachers and by students. These noble, unselfish young men and women gave expression to their love for the school, and loyally declared their intention to stand by it in its darkest hour. And in the weary weeks and months that followed before the building was replaced by another equally commodious and scarcely less beautiful, how faithfully was the pledge redeemed! Each realized that the continued existence of the great school depended in no small measure upon the affectionate loyalty of the student body.

Throughout Tuesday the work of selecting rooms and getting the necessary furniture went forward under the efficient direction of the resident trustee, Dr. James Roberts, assisted by a committee of citizens and professors. On Wednesday morning recitations were resumed in all departments. For many weeks the students without murmur tramped cheerfully down stairways and through snow from one poorly ventilated recitation room to another. Those who left to attend other schools could be counted upon the fingers. Thus, it will be observed, there had been but a single day's intermission in the work of the school. This remarkable fact, coupled with the striking loyalty exhibited by students and citizens, powerfully aided in securing an appropriation of one hundred and fifty-two thousand dollars from the next legislature.

The hour brings forth the man. Two years would elapse before the state could restore the burned structure. However loyal the students, they could not have been kept together in the uncomfortable quarters for such a length of time. The necessity of a temporary building was first realized by Mr. Isaac Rapp, the architect and builder, yet living in Carbondale. His brain conceived it, his hand brought it into being. Without consulting others he wrote the heading of a subscription paper for a temporary building. The business men of the town responded so generously that he had eighteen hundred dollars written down before the authorities of the school knew what he was doing. Of course his idea was enthusiastically adopted by them. The estimated cost of the building was thirty-five hundred dollars, but it was so easy to get subscriptions that Mr. Rapp's notion of what the building should be rapidly expanded so that when ready in January following for occupancy, it was a six thousand dollar structure. Erected during bitter December weather, the building could not be plastered. Instead of plaster the ceilings and walls of the different rooms were composed of thick brown paper tacked to the studding and the joists. And so in January, amid great rejoicing, the school moved into its new home thus quickly and generously provided by the citizens of Carbondale.

The Southern Normal had received its baptism of fire, but still lived stronger than before, supported by the love and loyalty of all. A new building in due time was reared upon the foundation of the old. Its halls and corridors have echoed to the feet of successive generations of students, who, whether they know it or not, owe a debt of gratitude to that gloriously unselfish group of four hundred young men and women of 1883, whose high devotion to duty preserved to the youth of Southern Illinois its Normal University.

Elegy On the Old Southern Normal.

MRS. CARRIE L. MOUNT.

Above, in the dome of the Heavens,
    Misty clouds so heavily creep;
Darkening as nearer the northward
    Where the cold breezes now sweep.

Frost gilded sidewalks and highways,
    Broad fields despoiled of their grain;
And trees with brown leaves, betoken
    That winter is now in his reign.

Beyond on a rise from the valley
    Apart from a white nestling town,
Stands a ruin—a giant-like structure,
    With its chimneys and walls falling down.

Around, in the spacious enclosure
    See evergreens stand here and there;
And winding among them neat pathways
    Lead up to the ruin so bare.

Ah! needs it to gaze but a moment
    To know that a fiery fiend
Has passed with his breath of destruction
    And the life of that edifice gleaned.

The roof lies low in the ashes,
    The casements are scorched with the flame;
The plastering and stairway have vanished
    And the front steps are hopelessly lame.

Heavy columns are leaning and bending,
    Great towers seem ready to fall;

High archways are tottering forward,
    Deep fissures appear in the wall.

I gaze on the scene that's before me,
    I wonder, I tremble, I weep:
For dear are the memories that hover
    Around that structureless heap.

Gone now from the casements, the windows,
    Bleak stand the skeleton walls;
Destroyed are the rooms full of beauty,
    Our much loved society halls.

Once they were teeming in gladness
    With the work of a far-famed school,
Whose scholars were models of perfection
    In the observance of duty and rule.

Once there were volumes of knowledge
    Set high in mighty array;
Once there were curious relics
    That were brought from climes far away.

Once there were lyceums of learning
    Unequaled by North or by South;
If ever they lacked in advancement
    'Twas due to an intellectual drouth.

But barring the weakness that's human,
    Of selfishness and her near sister pride,
There never were societies more friendly
    Than these, as they worked side by side.

And many the hearts that have quickened,
    And many the minds that have glowed,
And many the eyes that have brightened,
    And many the words that have flowed.

And many the tears that have sparkled,
    As gathered 'neath the gas burning light,
Some genius, in a first burst of passion,
    Battles strongly for truth and for right.

Down where there were compounds and mixtures
    Of gases and queer-smelling things,
Wise heads experimented and studied
    Acids, bases and phosphoric rings.

And so of each kind word and action,
    Of each principle skillfully taught,
The scene of the labor is over,
    But the results are eternally wrought.

Like fires that enkindle the Heavens,
    Like waters that continually sound,
The influence of the old Southern Normal
    Abroad in the earth shall be found.

And proud be the teacher and scholar
    Who have passed from the old to the new,
For theirs be the glory of proving
    That Egypt to her children is true.

January 31, 1884.

**LIBRARY
OF THE
UNIVERSITY OF ILLINOIS**

MAIN BUILDING.

History of Southern Illinois Normal Since 1883.

ON the morning of November 27, 1883, The Southern Illinois Normal was a school without a home. There were plenty of students, a competent faculty, good apparatus, a large library, but no house in which to put the material and to gather the students. Promptly the four churches offered their edifices for use as assembly halls, and the lawyers, doctors and editors tendered their offices for class-rooms. The kind offer was accepted; all began without delay to bring in the school furniture, to improvise shelves for library, and to construct cases for apparatus, while the generous hosts sought elsewhere for places of business for themselves. As the Baptist church was central to these class-rooms, it was used each morning for roll-call and opening exercises during our stay down town. Here announcements were made, visitors were received, and the school as a whole could be seen. After this, the students passed to the various places for recitations, or to their homes for study. Only two days were lost from regular class work after the fire.

The same promptness of decision and energy in reconstructing were shown by the members of the literary societies, as had been exhibited by the President and faculty. I have in my possession, among the many programs of the societies, one most valued as an index of the courage and energy of our young people. It consists of two leaves. On the first page is written:

INTER-SOCIETY PROGRAM,

SATURDAY EVENING, DECEMBER 1, 1883.

G. V. BUCHANAN,

PRESIDENT OF EVENING.

The two inside pages are blank, and on the fourth page is written:

. "HOMELESS, BUT NOT LIFELESS."

The account of this meeting will doubtless be given elsewhere; but the spirit it showed was a great encouragement to those who were working to keep the school together.

Although work was so speedily resumed, it was under great difficulties. So crowded were the rooms during recitation periods, it was impossible to set aside any place for the removal of wraps, or even to make a change of seats. During class time pupils wore their wraps, and those sitting near the stove endured the heat, while those at the back shivered with cold. No blackboards offered facilities for illustration; no desks allowed opportunities for examinations. It was a happy time for careless pupils.

As soon as the pressing need of immediate quarters had been met, the citizens of Carbondale turned their attention to providing a building which might keep together the normal school. The ladies gave a festival which lasted three days, by which they cleared $800. To this the friends added subscriptions until $6,000 was realized for the erection of a temporary home in the northwest corner of the normal campus. This was a small sum compared with the value of the house destroyed by the fire, but it was the free-will offering of a people heartily in sympathy with the institution, and determined that it should live. Under the able management of Mr.

Isaac Rapp as architect and builder, it was surprising how much comfort this sum obtained.

The temporary building was in the form of a Greek cross. The center was the study and assembly hall, a large room lighted by a skylight and four windows, one in each of the four spaces between the arms. In the arms were eleven class-rooms, the President's office and a room for the model school. No place could be set aside for the literary societies, but they used the largest two class-rooms for their meetings. With thankful hearts the school left the various offices down town on January 26, and moved into the temporary building so generously and so quickly provided. Granted it was far inferior to the former home; that the building, paper walls, were too light to stop elocution and music from becoming mixed with arithmetic and grammar; that the class-rooms were far too small; that the aisles in assembly hall were so narrow as to remind us of the "Fat Man's Misery" in Mammoth Cave; that even the skylight tower was crowded with property there stored; it was an improvement on down town, and a long step toward rebuilding. In spite of difficulties, patience and earnest purpose made the school year a success. At the first faculty meeting in the new quarters the following resolution was adopted:

RESOLUTIONS.

CARBONDALE, ILL., Feb. 4, 1884.

To the Principal and Faculty of The Southern Illinois Normal University:

Your committee appointed to prepare a resolution of thanks to the parties furnishing rooms for the use of the school in our time of great need, would submit the following;

Resolved, That the profound thanks of the faculty be heartily tendered to the following parties who so opportunly furnished us as instructors with rooms for recitation, assembly and storage purposes during the past two months; viz: Misses Haskell & Anthony, Col. D. H. B. Brush, C. W. Williams, Drs. F. M. & J. T. MacAnally, J. H. Caldwell, S. A. Dunaway, S. G. Hindman, J. M. Scurlock, W. H. Woodward, S. T. Brush, C. E. Brush, Messrs. Barr & Lemma, and Dr. James Robarts; also to the Trustees of the Baptist church and of St. Andrew's Mission.

Respectfully submitted,
C. W. Jerome, } Committee.
M. A. Raymond, }

Gradually we became accustomed to our new surroundings, and the work moved forward steadily. Some even declared they liked our crowded condition, as it was so much more social. Lunches were eaten in groups in the various class rooms; these were called hotels and you might hear such remarks as, "The Jerome House furnishes toothpicks. let us patronize that." Commencement of 1884 drew nigh. Now arose a question of great importance, and it must be decided quickly. No hall in town could hold the people who would attend the Commencement exercises. Our assembly hall was crowded when only the school was present, so it was out of the question to try to use it for the general audiences. The public had always been welcomed, and we were desirous of having all come in this, our hour of adversity. The students remained faithful to the school, and a good class was to be graduated; this would bring many visitors from a distance. After careful consideration, it seemed best to obtain a large tent in which to hold the week's exercises.

The use of a tent gave rise to many jokes on the

seniors by the under-graduates; they persisted in calling it a circus, and assigning absurd parts to the various members of the graduating class as the animals in the show, and to the faculty as constituting the company. This comical view of the situation was only the white cap upon the great wave of earnestness and good will with which all worked to make the exercises a success. At almost any time in the day Professor Brownlee could be seen under a large tree in the grove west of the campus, aiding some prospective orator to prepare for Commencement day or for one of the society entertainments. Early and late, sounds harmonious and discordant, issued from Professor Inglis' room, where he trained the singers for the approaching gala days. All seemed anxious to do well and show to the world that the school yet lived, though its shell had been destroyed.

Unfortunately for the use of the tent, Commencement week opened with strong indications of storm. Monday evening was the time for the annual entertainment by the undergraduates of the Socratic Literary Society. Undaunted by the threatening weather, the people came and filled the tent. The program was about one-third completed when the storm broke, accompanied by a furious wind, which extinguished the lights, while the noise of the rain upon the canvas almost extinguished the speakers. As the lights went out Richard T. Lightfoot was giving an oration. He paused until a lantern could be lit and put upon the platform; then in clear tones and perfect self-possession resumed the line of thought and completed the oration before an audience sitting in darkness. Spirits that had risen above the fire could not be conquered by the storm. By this time the wind was less strong, the lamps were lit and the program could be completed as intended. Next night the moon illumined all the campus as the happy Zetetics gave their exercises untroubled by the fury of Æolus.

Thursday was clear and hot; it was evident that old Sol would be present and have a warm interest in the proceedings. His smile was so bright upon our canvas roof that all eyes were dazzled. Look where you would— at audience, faculty, class, or orators—every one was squinting and smiling; the facial expression can better be imagined than described. Soon the heat became oppressive; white dresses hung limp on perspiring shoulders and high collars passed out of fashion. However, speakers overcame all difficulties, and all trials were cheerfully endured, as hope pictured before us the spacious new building which Illinois should cause to rise Phœnix-like from the ashes of the old. Three years later this dream was realized.

The fall of '84 was looked forward to with great apprehension by those who desired the rebuilding of the normal. After the fire the body of students remained and were an unanswerable argument in favor of its continuation; now it was very doubtful whether new pupils would come in to fill the places vacated by the many who each year begin the work of teaching without waiting to complete the course. It scarcely seemed reasonable to expect that young people who were strangers to the institution would choose to enter a school where so poor accommodations were to be had when at the same expense they could find so much better elsewhere. This was the true crisis in the life of the Southern Normal. If the year opened with greatly reduced numbers, a spirit of restlessness and dissatisfaction would be apt to appear, which would be detrimental to good work. This would result in the loss of the best students, and ultimately in ruin to the school.

During the summer months the members of the faculty worked in county institutes even more than usual, thus making many new friends for the institution they represented. Yet it was with much foreboding that we approached the time for beginning the eleventh year. The first day set all fears at rest, as old students returned from the various counties, bringing their friends with them to enter upon a course of study. Their bright, hopeful faces dispelled all doubt, and the work of the year was begun in a spirit of confidence that the life of the school was assured.

In this year some of the most trying features of our hastily built home had been removed. Plaster had replaced paper on the walls, so the sounds from one class did not impede the work of its neighbor. The floors had been rendered warmer by boxing up the open space below the house, so pupils no longer found it necessary to wear overshoes all day, as in the previous winter. The time passed quickly, filled with incidents laughable and perplexing, but cheered by favorable reports of the progress of the bill asking for an appropriation for rebuilding. This was finally passed by our legislature, and received Governor Oglesby's signature June 25, 1885. If it had passed in time for Commencement the enthusiasm would have been unbounded.

The twelfth year opened bright with promise. Again new students came in good numbers to fill the places of those who could not return. Classes were large and enthusiastic, for from the windows could be seen men working on the ruins, cleaning away the debris from the uninjured foundation, upon which was to be erected a new and better home for the Southern Normal. Plans for the new building were the topic of greatest interest; and although it was evident it could not be ready this year, hope pictured it so vividly that the inconveniences of the present were unnoticed, as all enjoyed in imagination the comforts and delights of the future. This buoyancy of faith was one of the best possible illustrations of what the Apostle Paul pictures for the Christian in Corinthians 4:-18. Commencement passed in the tent with the usual incidents, and all went to their homes determined to bring with them the next September as many as possible to share the advantages offered by the new building.

Slowly, it seemed to the waiting school, did the new building near completion; so great a work requires time if it be well done. It was not until February 24, 1887, that the trustees received the edifice, and it was dedicated with appropriate ceremonies, having been built within the limit of the sum granted. The next Monday it was ready for the happy faculty and students to take possession.

At first they felt lost in the great hall for study and assembly. Here, from some positions, their voices called forth echoes which proved very annoying. To remedy this Professor Rocheleau some years later draped cloth from the ceiling near the rear of the hall; it's pretty light green color harmonized well with the frescoes above, and by it the echoes were restrained. As time passed the green faded, and before its removal the drapery became known by the absurd name of "Pa Rocheleau's washing."

Commencement of 1887 was largely attended; seventeen hundred people were seated in the new assembly hall to enjoy the exercises and to rejoice in the prosperity of Egypt's normal school. Having held its own while passing through the years of adversity, it is not surprising that the school now entered upon a period of established increase in numbers and influence. It has never been subject to a "boom;" but like the corn of the land in which it is situated, it has attained its present size by a constant and healthy growth.

As the years passed, the roll of alumni increased. Returning to manifest their allegiance to their Alma Mater as opportunity offered, they noticed with sorrow that the time was fast approaching when Dr. Allyn would no longer be there to welcome home his boys and girls. A strong desire to obtain a large picture of him, to be placed in the parlor of the normal, culminated in 1889 by inducing him to sit for his portrait while on a visit to the east. It was painted by the artist-hand of J. Conant, of life-size, and was given to the normal by the Alumni Association at Commencement in 1891. It now looks from the walls of the parlor with so life-like an expression that old students feel at home as they behold the well-remembered form. None too soon was this step taken, for three years later Dr. Allyn had passed away. When the Columbian Exposition drew nigh, the Southern Illinois Normal, true to its progressive policy, took a prominent part in preparing the educational exhibits of the state. The plans were laid and the work begun in the last year of Dr. Allyn's administration, and successfully carried out the year Professor Hull was at the head. The exhibits being ready and space assigned our school in the Illinois state building, some one must be put in charge who could intelligently answer questions on the work. It was the unanimous wish of the faculty that the position be so filled as to assist the greatest possible number of our students to visit the exposition and enjoy its educational advantages. It was decided to put two in charge at a time, each to stay four weeks, but so to appoint that one change came every two weeks. By this arrangement was assured one who was conversant with the exhibit as company for each new man. There being two at a time, every one had opportunity to use half his time in other parts of the Fair, and yet not leave our work without some one to welcome those who called at S. I. N. U. headquarters.

Our cases were arranged around the sides of the space allotted us, thus forming in the center a pretty room; here were put chairs, desk, writiting material and other comforts for the convenience of friends who called. It made a delightful home for Southern Illinois people who were visiting the great exposition. The praise and awards received by our school exhibit were very gratifying to the people of Egypt. At the close of the Fair the cases and matter were brought home, and are now a part of the material used in the departments to which they belong.

The World's Fair exhibits gave an impetus to the teaching of science in public schools. Many high schools added laboratory work to their old requirements in textbook study. This increased demand made it necessary that our students should have better facilities for preparation while with us than could be afforded by class-rooms, museum, and one laboratory. A plain statement of our needs was made to the legislature in 1895, and an appropriation of $40,000 was granted for the erection of a building to be used for science work and as a library. This house was completed, as usual, within the limits of the appropriation, and was dedicated to the purposes of education. It contains a gymnasium, four class-rooms, and a library. The better facilities for pursuing studies in science bring many teachers for post-graduate work during the summer months. This is now done with a thoroughness of which the school may well be proud.

Smoothly has the work gone forward till now it is with surprise we come to our silver anniversary; it is a time of union and prosperity. Within the school all work harmoniously under the leadership of our friend and president, Dr. D. B. Parkinson. He has been in the faculty from the first, and knows how to deal with the different dispositions there represented. His twenty-five years of efficient service have endeared him to the people of Southern Illinois. In every town many of its prominent citizens have been his pupils, and now exert an influence in favor of the school. The formation of the School Council last year has brought into closer union the educational forces of Egypt, for whose uplifting all willingly labor. As we look out we see, not a setting sun casting its radiance on our section of the state, but behold the sun approaching its meridian splendor. Happy are the teachers who shall henceforth labor in this glorious field!

Our Trustees—Past and Present.

SOON after the approval of the act of the Legislature that created the Southern Illinois Normal University, Governor John M. Palmer appointed a Board of Trustees, who were to carry into effect the articles of the act or charter in locating the school and erecting suitable buildings. These Charter Trustees, as they were afterward called, were:

Capt. Daniel Hurd of Cairo.
Gen. Eli Boyer of Olney.
Col. Thomas M. Harris of Shelbyville.
Rev. Elihu J. Palmer of Bellville.
Samuel Flannigan, Esq., of Benton.

The Board was appointed in 1869. The Trustees entered upon their duties, sought bids from various towns in the region south of the Ohio and Mississippi Railroad and after locating the school at Carbondale, let the contract to Mr. James M. Campbell to erect a building. Work was begun in the spring of 1870 and the corner stone of the new building was laid May 17th of that year. Work progressed till by an accident Mr. Campbell lost his life in the spring of 1871.

Mr. Palmer moved from Belleville to Carbondale where he might more easily look after the interests of the building that was in progress.

On the death of Mr. Campbell work on the building stopped and nothing more was done till the Legislature, then in session, by a new act approved April 15, 1871, created a new Board and carried the work on under con-

S. P. WHEELER.

A. C. BROOKINGS.

ALFRED BAYLISS.

D. W. HELM.

**LIBRARY
OF THE
UNIVERSITY OF ILLINOIS**

ditions different from those under which it was started. The new act provided for the appointment of three men known as Building Commissioners, who were to have charge of the completion of the work at Carbondale. Also of the new Insane Asylum that was being built at Anna. The act provided for three Commissioners, two of whom were to be practical builders of whom one was to take charge of the work at Anna and the other at Carbondale, while the third was to be Secretary and Treasurer of the Board. Besides these three the writer finds three other names in the lists as afterwards published. The new Board of Building Commissioners are:

Hiram Walker, Jonesboro.

R. H. Sturgess, Vandalia.

F. M. Malone, Pana.

John Wood, Cairo.

Rev. Elihu J. Palmer, Carbondale.

Nathan Bishop, Marion.

The first three of these appended their names to the report to the Governor that was sent to the Senate May 4, 1873, and hence served to be the part of the Board officially responsible for the erection of the buildings at Anna and Carbondale and the expenditure of the funds donated by the State and the two towns.

Under an act that was approved May 2, 1873, a set of five Trustees was appointed whose duty it was to take charge of the building as soon as the Building Commissioners were through with their work, and proceeded to furnish the building in accordance with the original act, and make other provisions for opening of the school. The following are the first Trustees as appointed by Gov-, ernr John L. Beveridge.

Hon. Thos. S. Ridgeway, Shawneetown.

Dr. James Robarts, Carbondale.
Edwin S. Russell, Mt. Carmel.
Lewis M. Phillips, Nashville.
Jacob W. Wilkins, Marshall.

Of this Board Mr. Ridgeway was chosen President, and Dr. Robarts Secretary. Mr. Ridgeway remained President of the Board till his retirement from it in 1893, and Dr. Roberts until he was succeeded as a member of the Board by E. J. Ingersoll in 1895. The other officers of this first Board were John G. Campbell, Treasurer and Prof. Charles W. Jerome, Registrar. Mr. Campbell was succeeded as Treasurer by Mr. John Bridges in 1878. Professor Jerome remained Registrar until he retired from the Faculty in 1890, when Prof. John Hull was appointed as his successor.

Of this first Board three were more personally known to the writer than the others. Hon. T. S. Ridgeway was a banker at his home in Shawneetown and had served as State Treasurer. Dr. Robarts was a prominent physician and surgeon in Carbondale and had served as surgeon in the army during the war of the rebellion. Mr. L. M. Phillips was a lawyer of note in Nashville.

On the death of Mr. Phillips Prof. Samuel M. Inglis, Superintendent of the Schools of Greenville, was appointed March 25, 1891, as his successor, his term to expire in March, 1883. Upon the expiration of his term as Trustee he was elected to the chair of Algebra and Arithmetic, taking his seat as a member of the Faculty with the opening of the fall term, 1883.

In 1882 two new members were added to the Board. These were Cicero R. Hughes, of Cairo, to succeed Edwin S. Russell, and Dr. Henry C. Fairbrother, of East St. Louis, to succeed Jacob W. Wilkins. When Professor Inglis' term expired Governor Hamilton sent in the name of Isaac B. Self as his successor, but there does not appear to be any record of his confirmation by the Senate. The one who did take his place was R. D. Adams of Fairfield. The Board as published in the Catlogue of 1893-4 is:

Hon. Thos. S. Ridgeway, Shawneetown.
Dr. James Robarts, Carbondale.
Cicero N. Hughes, Cairo.
Dr. Henry C. Fairbrother, East St. Louis.
R. D. Adams, Fairfield.

The next year, 1885, Ezekiel J. Ingersol, of Carbondale, was appointed to the place of Resident Trustee, held up to this time by Dr. Robarts. Mr. Ingersoll held this place till Governor Altgeld, in 1893, made a change in the personel of the Board. With Mr. Ingersoll was also appointed Hon. Samuel P. Wheeler, of Cairo, who succeeded Cicero N. Hughes, of the same place.

In the revision of the school law the Legislature of 1889 made it one of the duties of State Superintendent of Public Instruction to be Ex-officio Trustee of the Southern Illinois Normal University, as set forth in Article 16 of the Enumeration of His Duties. This brought Hon. Richard Edwards in as a member of the Board for the year 1889-90. The Board had two others changes that year, standing as follows:

Hon. Thos. S. Ridgeway, Shawneetown.
E. J. Ingersoll, Carbondale.
Hon. Samuel J. Wheeler, Springfield.
Emil Schmidt, Nashville.
Edward C. Fitch, Albion.
Hon. Richard Edwards, Springfield, ex-officio.
And S. T. Brush was chosen Treasurer by the Board.

The only change that is to be noted next year is the name of Hon. Henry Raab, the ex-officio Trustee, by virtue of his election to the office of Superintendent of Public Instruction in place of Hon. Richard Edwards. This year Prof. John Hull succeeded Prof. Jerome as Registrar.

Two years later, in 1893, when Hon. J. P. Altgeld was inaugurated Governor, Mr. Ridgeway's term expired by limitation, and Mr. Schmidt's death caused another vacancy in the Board. The resignation of the remaining three members was asked for and the entire personnel of the Board was changed, with the exception of Hon. Henry Raab, who, as State Superintendent, was ex-officio member. The new Board was:

C. W. Bliss, Hillsboro.
J. W. Terry, Edwardsville.
E. C. Baughman, Olney.
W. R. Ward, Benton.
S. W. Dunaway, Carbondale.

The new Board chose Mr. Bliss as President, and Mr. Ward as Secretary, and elected J. M. Evans Treasurer.

There was no further change in the Board till 1895, when C. W. Terry, a son of J. W. Terry, was appointed to a place on the Board in place of his father.

The election of 1804 placed Prof. S. M. Inglis in the State Superintendent's office in place of Mr. Raab, and this brought him into the Board of Trustees again, but this time as member ex-officio, by virtue of his office at Springfield.

Two years later the election of 1896 changed the State administration, Governor John R. Tanner taking the place of the outgoing Governor, J. P. Altgeld. In

F. A. PRICKETT.

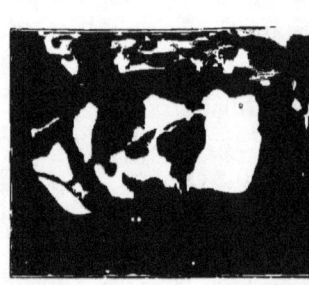

F. C. VANDERVORT.

T. O. JOHNSTON.

**LIBRARY
OF THE
UNIVERSITY OF ILLINOIS**

the matter of the Trustees of this school Governor Tanner followed the example of his predecessor and appointed new men in place of the old Board. The Board that was appointed the spring of 1897 was:

Hon. S. P. Wheeler, Springfield.
Col. F. A. Prickett, Carbondale.
Dr. A. C. Brookings, Du Quoin.
D. W. Helm, Esq., Metropolis.
T. O. Johnston, Oregon; with
Hon. S. M. Inglis, Springfield, ex-officio.

At their first meeting the new Board elected Mr. Wheeler President, and Mr. Prickett Secretary, and appointed E. K. Porter to be Treasurer, The only change that has been made in this Board is the appointment just before the close of the session, of Dr. F. C. Vandervoort, of Bloomington, in place of T. O. Johnston, of Oregon, recently deceased. The election of a new State Superintendent, Hon. Alfred Bayliss, adds also his name to the new Board in place of Hon. S. M. Inglis.

On the appointment of Professor John Hull to the head of the Faculty, in 1892, Professor D. B. Parkinson became his successor in the Registrar's office, a place he held 'till he was appointed President of the school, when Professor H. W. Shryock was appointed to the office of Registrar by the Board.

Of the Trustees who have had charge of the school six have died, two after the expiration of their term of office, and four while in office. The first of these was Mr. L. M. Phillips, during the Christmas holidays of 1880. The second was Mr. Emil Schmidt, who died February 2, 1893. The third Superintendent, S. M. Inglis, died June 1, 1878. The fourth was Mr. T. O. Johnston, who died April 4, 1899. The other two, who died after the expiration of their term of office, were: Dr. James Robarts, July 24, 1890, and Hon. T. S. Ridgeway, November 18, 1897.

It might be of interest here to say that Governor Tanner offered Mr. Ridgeway the position of Trustee, a position he had held from the beginning of the school, with the exception of four years, but he declined, as he felt his health was not such as to justify him in assuming again the responsibility.

It might be said, also, that some time during the winter of 1897–'98 Mr. Rodney D. Adams met with an accident from a fall that, while not causing his death, resulted in injuries from which he has not recovered.

The following is a tabulated list of the men who have served as Trustees of the Southern Illinois Normal University, the year of their appointment and when they retired:

	Appointed.	Retired.
*Hon. T. S. Ridgeway, Shawneetown	1873	1893
*Dr. James Robarts, Carbondale	1873	1884
Edwin S. Russell, Mt. Carmel	1873	1883
*Lewis M. Phillips, Nashville	1873	1880
Jacob W. Wilkins, Marshall	1873	1883
*Hon. Samuel M. Inglis, Greenville	1881	1883
Cicero N. Hughes, Cairo	1883	1885
Dr. Henry C. Fairbrother, East St. Louis	1883	1889
Rodney D. Adams, Fairfield	1883	1889
Ezekiel J. Ingersoll, Carbondale	1885	1893
Hon. Samuel P. Wheeler, Cairo	1885	1893
*Emil Schmidt, Nashville	1889	1893
Edward C. Fitch, Albion	1889	1893
Hon. Richard Edwards, Ex-officio	1889	1891
Hon. Henry Raab, Ex-officio	1891	1895
C. W. Bliss, Hillsboro	1893	1897
J. W. Terry, Edwardsville	1893	1895
E. C. Bauhman, Olney	1893	1897
W. R. Ward, Benton	1893	1897
S. W. Dunaway, Carbondale	1893	1897
C. W. Terry, Edwardsville	1895	1897
*Hon. S. M. Inglis, Ex.officio	1895	1898

	Appointed.	Retired.
Hon. S. P. Wheeler, Springfield	1897	
Col. F. A. Prickett, Carbondale	1897	
Dr. A. C. Brookings, Du Quoin	1897	
D. W. Helm, Metropolis	1897	
*T. O. Johnson, Oregon	1897	1899
Hon. Alfred Bayliss, Ex-officio	1899	
Dr. F. C. Vandervoort, Bloomington	1899	

*Deceased.

The Influence of the S. I. S. N. U.

FOR one to attempt an estimate of the influence of a school in which he himself has a part is a somewhat difficult task; but the writer of the aftergoing article has been connected with the Southern Illinois State Normal for so short a time, and has had so little to do either with determining the policy of the school, or developing its methods, that he feels that he will be acquitted of boastfulness, even though he speaks somewhat strongly concerning the school and its work. The writer would like to have it remembered, too, that he is an Egyptian, and that what he has herein set down with regard to the schools of Southern Illinois of twenty-five years ago is written in no spirit of captiousness; but to understand what the influence of the Southern Normal has been, it is necessary for us to know what the school conditions were when it began its work.

Many causes co-operated to hold in check the educational work in the southern part of the state. The majority of the settlers came from the slave-holding states, where public education in its modern sense was yet undreamt of. When the emigrants from Kentucky and Tennessee broke away from their old homes and turned their faces toward the northwest, it was not so much that they might find better and cheaper lands, as it was that they might find better educational and social advantages. Our forefathers perhaps formulated their reasons for leaving their old homes in the somewhat vague phrase, "We can do better in Illinois." But whether formulated or

SCIENCE BUILDING.

**LIBRARY
OF THE
UNIVERSITY OF ILLINOIS**

not, there was undoubtedly an underlying conviction that they were escaping from a land that for the poor, at least, had nothing better than intellectual bondage, to a region that gave promise of intellectual freedom. So it came to pass that almost as soon as they were settled in their new homes they began to build school houses and in an earnest, thoug hcrude, way to strive for better things.

A school, however, is an organism of slow growth. The higher institutions of learning, the great universities, which, mountain-like, send down a benison of dews and vitalizing showers upon the intellectual lowlands, had not yet upreared themselves. The colleges of Southern Illinois were doing a noble but insufficient work. Earnest and able as were the men who wrought in Shurtleff and McKendree, there was an abiding reason why they could not do the work of uplifting the public schools of the southern part of the state. The young man who entered Shurtleff or McKendree did so for the purpose of fitting himself for the law, journalism, medicine, or the ministry. He might teach a term or two to help pay the expenses of his college course, but scarcely one in a hundred ever dreamed of making teaching his profession. Here and there one who had begun to teach for the mere purpose of tiding over the interval until he could hope to make a living by the practice of law, or some other profession, found himself in love with his temporary vocation and decided to make it his life-work; but such an one was the rare exception. It is evident, of course, that a college-bred man must always exert a wholesome influence upon the community in which he lives; but so far as the public schools are concerned the influence of the educated man in any profession other than teaching, must always be more largely indirect than otherwise. As a consequence the influence of the college is almost imperceptible in the public school. The State Normal at Normal, Illinois, had already begun to do a noble work in the cause of popular education; but the influence of any school is largely local, and it is doubtful if ten per cent. of the teachers of Southern Illinois had ever even heard of the old State Nornal.

And thus it was that down to a period as late as twenty-five years ago the work of the public schools in this section continued to be lamentably crude. At the date alluded to there were only three high schools south of the Vandalia Railroad, and, measured by our present standard, not one of these maintained more than a three-years course. The work in the district school was almost inconceivably crude and chaotic. An accurate description of the work done in even the best of the country schools of the period reads almost like a caricature,

Let me sketch briefly, but as acurately as possible, one of the better grades of the country school of something like thirty years ago. A weatherbeaten, dilapidated building, twenty by thirty, with a ceiling nine feet in height, sheltered, after a fashion, forty or fifty pupils of all ages. No classification was attempted, and no effort was made to have any uniformity of text books. Each pupil took whatsoever studies he chose to take, or that his parents chose to have him take. Spelling, reading, geography, arithmetic, and a nondescript exercise called writing made up the course of study. In the school being described there were at one time two boys who fancied that they were studying grammar; one used Pinneo as a text, and the other used Clark. The writer well remembers with what evident pride, and yet misgiving, the teacher used to summon to the recitation end of the room these two earnest seekers after etymological and syntactical truth. While these two budding linguists were strenuously wrestling with pronouns, participles and the like, or with reckless hands inscribing "bologna-sausage" diagrams on the neutral-colored pine board, called by courtesy a black-board, the other pupils would suspend all their ordinary tasks to stare at these prodigies of learning, and to "wonder with a foolish face of praise." Now and then a pupil would boldly attack history, but such conduct was usually looked upon as reprehensible. On one occasion an audacious youth presented himself, text-book in hand, and asked to be assigned a lesson in physiology. The teacher took the book, opened it, turned slowly through its pages, finally handed it back, and in a tone that was meant to be bitingly sarcastic, said "I guess you've made a mistake; this hain't no school for doctors."

From the above description of one of the best of the country schools of the period it is not hard to infer what must have been the character of the worst. Log school houses, with their puncheon floors and rough-hewn benches, were not uncommon; and the course of study and the character of the instruction were, more often than otherwise, on the farther side of the farcical.

Such were the conditions when, twenty-five years ago, the twelve earnest men and women composing the first faculty took up the work of elevating the standard of popular education in Southern Illinois. I need not take time to describe the conditions as they exist to-day, after twenty-five years of unremitting labor. Those who do institute work, or attend teachers' meetings in all parts of the state, know that there is no section where there is more uniformly excellent work done than in these southern counties. While I have no disposition to disparage the value of other influences that have been at work to promote this almost marvelous progress, yet I believe we may justly claim that, after all, the chief factor has been this professional school with its high ideals.

The very establishment of the Normal was a declaration that teaching was henceforth to be regarded as a profession; and when once the public had accepted this truth, the battle was half-won; and it was not many years until the school had made good its declaration by sending out a small army to support and spread the doctrine of professionalism.

To understand how strong this army has grown to be, let us examine briefly the official records of the school.

The total number enrolled has now reached nearly seven thousand. The average length of time spent in the school is about sixty weeks. Of the total number enrolled some paid tuition and were not required to take the pledge to teach. A small number took the pledge, but failed to keep the obligation imposed therein. After making allowance for these two classes, however, there still remain more than six thousand who have taught long enough, at least, to satisfy the obligation; and out of the number there are hundreds who have made teaching a life work. Our graduates are filling some of the best school positions in the state. During the past year the superintendencies in fourteen of the best cities of Southern Illinois, and a number of county superintendencies, as well as the best places in many of the best high schools, were held by Southern Normal graduates. In all, ten have been called to important places in the Normal itself, and some are holding high positions in other states.

Year by year the school has grown in equipment and

in influence, until to-day it offers splendid opportunities for professional training; stately buildings, fully equipped chemical, physical and biological laboratories, a library of fourteen thousand volumes, sixteen professors, a special training department in the hands of experts—these form the equipment which has been developed here for the training of those who desire to teach. With the increase in our facilities for doing work, and with the growth of a professional spirit among the school men of our section of the state, there has grown up a feeling that Carbondale is the educational center for Southern Illinois. In proof of this assertion it might be noted that three of the most widely known school organizations in the state, the Southern Illinois, High School Athletic and Oratorical Association, the Southern Illinois Teachers' Association, and the School Council of Illinois have held their annual meetings at Carbondale. One of these organizations has made Carbondale its permanent home, and another has made a move in the same direction.

Thus far I have spoken of the influences of the Normal as reflected in the schools of the region that it was designed to serve, but the larger effect of its influence must be sought for in the life of the people. It is always difficult to tell how far any one factor influences the sum total of the life of a people; still I think we may fairly claim that the Southern Normal has contributed much to the development of the manhood and womanhood of Southern Illinois; for through the six thousand workers who have received their training in its halls, and have then gone out to do their work, the school has laid its quickening touch upon the life of every nook and corner of this part of the state.

Our Presidents.

ROBERT ALLYN, LL. D.

NEW ENGLAND'S greatest contribution to the nation is not manufactured cotton, nor the printing press, nor the newspaper, nor even the university, but the noble, stalwart men she has produced. In the quality of her sons she has enriched the world. Their moral and intellectual fiber has given strength and stability to American character. Their lofty ideals, their unselfish purposes, their exalted patriotism, their tireless energy, their intelligent and intense devotion to duty, have in no small degree influenced our nationality. It is no vain statement to say that the New Englanders have ever been among the pioneers of progress, and have ably assisted in directing the course of events on this continent.

The Plymouth colonists, the founders of Boston and the early settlers of the Connecticut valley, were people of humble birth and surroundings—of simple manners and generous impulses. Their chief wealth consisted not in gold, nor landed estates, nor slaves, but in practical intelligence and persevering industry. They also had in a marked degree an exalted sense of honor, profound convictions, and magnificent courage. Their descendants for several generations have been men and women of heroic mold, of forceful personalities in private and public affairs.

Nature has not been so luxuriantly bountiful in New England as in more southern latitudes of this country.

With unfavorable agricultural conditions, such as sterile soil and adverse climate, the natural resources were necessarily limited. But the early New Englanders were not to be discouraged, and their inventive genius and indomitable will eventually surmounted all obstacles to their advancement. The commercial instinct was aroused and various employments were created. The forests were cleared and the lumber sold abroad or exchanged for the products of other colonies; extensive fisheries were established for a thousand miles along the coast; swift streams and rivers were utilized for milling, and towns by the hundred sprang up and became the centers of manufacuring and commercial activity.

This experience of struggling with the stern conditions which confronted them, and adapting themselves to their peculiar environments, contributed no small part to the formation of that sturdy and truly remarkable character for which the New Englander has ever been noted. Patience, self-reliance and heroic strength came through conquering difficulties, and were a rich legacy to the generations that have since made New England famous.

During all this period of industrial expansion, the cultivation of the ennobling virtues was not neglected. The lessons of honesty, sobriety, truthfulness, love of knowledge, and respect for the rights of others, were taught by precept and example. Puritan intolerance gave way to liberty of conscience and the spirit of brotherhood, as taught by Roger Williams. The religious element in New England life has always been prominent, and its growth and influence have not been retarded by political and social hindrances. Here, indeed, has the church been a tower of strength in influencing individual character and shaping public policies.

Next to religion, education has been prized by the people of New England. In this sphere of activity substantial progress was made in colonial days. Educational needs were early recognized, and colleges were established that have steadily grown in usefulness and power. Harvard, Yale, Dartmouth, Wesleyan, Bowdoin, Brown, Williams and Amherst all flourished as centers of intellectual light in New England. Later on the public school system was organized and has exerted a commanding influence in the nation. The normal school idea, which has revolutionized educational methods, had its inception in the brain of Horace Mann, a typical New Englander, a man of noble character, and an educator of great renown.

His friend and co-worker, Robert Allyn, the subject of this sketch, was a descendant of the best New England stock, his ancestors being primarily of English blood. He was eminently well-born. The intelligence, high purpose and genuine piety of a score of generations were his inheritance. Those personal traits so characteristic of the cultured and refined people of the eastern states, and which had been developed and nurtured by decades of disciplinary experience peculiar to the time and locality, were his in extraordinary measure.

Born at Ledyard, New London county, Conn., January 25, 1817, his boyhood was spent on the farm and his early education was gained in the public schools. He loved study, and while very young formed the habit of reading good books, many of which were procured from the town library of his native place. Even when a boy he read with intelligent interest the standard books of literature, and the impressions received from this source were lasting and effective. This habit, doubtless, had much to do with the formation of his character, as it created new ideals, enriched his thought, stimulated his imagination, and enlarged his mental horizon. A well sustained public library is a reliable intellectual pulse of a community. Like the public school, and the college, its blessings are not only immediate but far-reaching in their influence. The college libraries of New England were pioneers in fostering a love for literature, and there the trend of many a grand career received its first direction and impulse.

Supplementing his educational attainments by one year's study at Bacon Academy in the neighboring town of Colchester, he began his life work of teaching at the age of seventeen in East Lynn within his native county. After teaching one year he entered Wesleyan Academy at Wilbraham, Mass., where he finished his preparation for college. In 1837, being twenty years of age, he began his college course at Wesleyan University, Middletown, Conn., where he pursued his studies for four years, graduating with distinction in 1841. He was especially commended for his acquirements in methaphysics and mathematics.

His Alma Mater is a prominent institution of learning and many of her graduates have been and are among the most talented and representative men of the nation. Bishops, educators, editors, senators, governors and jurists belong to this noted galaxy of great men. Middletown may justly be called the cradle of educational methodism in America. Syracuse, Northwestern, and De Pauw Universities, McKendree College and the "Wesleyans" of Ohio, Illinois, Iowa and Kansas, are the offspring of this venerable institution.

Immediately after graduation, having been elected to the professorship of mathematics in Wilbraham Academy, where he had fitted himself for college, he accepted the position for which he was so admirably prepared. He filled this chair very acceptably till his resignation two years later to enter the ministry.

Having joined the Methodist church two years before entering college, and designing to spend his life in the ministry, much of his study had been along theological lines. He devoted himself almost exclusively to ministerial work for two years, preaching at Colchester, Conn., when he was recalled to Wilbraham Academy— this time as its honored head. He served in this capacity three years with marked ability. This was his first executive experience in educational work. His success here showed that leadership was his forte, and determined the line along which he was to win his laurels in future years.

He next accepted the presidency of a Methodist Academy in East Greenwich, R. I. His labors there covered a period of six years and gave eminent satisfaction. He also served two terms in the legislature of this state.

Dr. Allyn now stood in the front ranks as an educator and was honored with the office of State Superintendent of Public Instruction of Rhode Island, where he attained great distinction by his three and a half years of service. In 1857, at the age of forty, he came West to Ohio, and assumed the professorship of ancient languages in Ohio University at Athens, where he remained two years and resigned to accept the presidency of Wesleyan Female College in Cincinnati. After four years successful labor in this field, he was elected president of McKendree College, Lebanon, Ill.

So, in the maturity of his powers and the height of

his reputation he came to give the balance of his long life and able efforts to the cause of education in our much loved state of Illinois. He remained in Lebanon eleven years, from 1863 to 1874. Here his strong personality infused new life into the institution and resulted in more than doubling both the attendance and the endowment of the college. The marked success of his labors attracted the attention of the leading educators of the state, and he was selected as first president of the Southern Illinois Normal University, which had just been established at Carbondale. Thenceforth he was our own till "God took him." For twenty years he went in and out amongst us—an elevating and beneficent influence for good.

His personal character was lofty and pure, his thought profound and broad, his conversation instructive, elegant and chaste. He was a man of high ideals, of tender sentiment, of strong intellectual endowments. The breadth of his thought and the wide range of his mental capabilities were remarkable.

Much of his greatness lay in the versatility of his powers. He was a clear and vigorous writer, using always the purest English, imparting to his productions a scholarly and stately style which was much admired. As a preacher and lecturer he impressed the public with his deep learning and genuine moral worth. Long will his baccalaureate sermons be remembered by the hundreds of students who have heard them. Many of his printed sermons might be called masterpieces of literature, abounding in grand thought and exalted sentiment. Whether in the pulpit, on the lecture platform, or as a contributor to newspapers and magazines, he always expressed himself in the refinements of rhetoric. As a teacher he realized the great dignity and responsibility of his profession. His rich stores of knowledge, coupled with an ardent love for young manhood and womanhood, created in the school a benign and invigorating atmosphere. From his daily readings he constantly gave to his pupils the best thoughts of the greatest men. He was able to bring out the essential features of a subject in a logical and orderly manner, placing facts and principles before his students with clearness and force. His long experience in dealing with the young gave him a full understanding of youthful nature, and his abundant patience with the shortcomings and blunders incident to immature judgment and the impetuosity of youth, endeared him to the hearts of his pupils. He had the rare faculty of knowing all the students under his care, and of remembering names and faces always. His warm grasp of the hand and kindly word of sympathy, or interest, sent a glow to the heart and a light to the eye of many a struggling youth and maiden. Deliberate and persistent wrong doing found in him no apologist nor defender. His "righteous wrath" against evil exhibited the strong force of his character quite as fully as did his love of the good and pure. Toward his associate teachers he was always courteous and just, thoughtful of their interests, and helpful in their work. Never dictatorial nor despotic, he gave to each his due mead of appreciation and praise.

He possessed administrative talents of high order, and in his strong hand the machinery of government worked with but little friction. Of commanding presence and possessing in a rare degree the dignity of true manliness, his fitness for authority and leadership was never questioned.

Dr. Allyn had a comprehensive grasp of affairs. His foresight was statesmanlike—so keen and penetrating that it amounted almost to prophecy. He was in the fore-front not only in recognizing the educational needs of the state, but in seeing the possibility of supplying them. Twenty years ago he advocated the establishment of five normal schools in Illinois; and to-day we see the fruition of his wise counsel in the legislative acts of recent years providing for three new normal schools in addition to the two already organized.

He was a member of the National Educational Association, and also of the National Council of Education, whose membership was limited to sixty of the most active and prominent educators of the nation.

His educational career was wrought out in five states, and covered the exceptionally long period of more than half a century. His acquaintance was necessarily extensive, and his student friends are to be found in nearly every state in the Union, and in some countries across the sea.

Having passed his seventy-fifth birthday, he retired from active labor, carrying with him to his quiet home-life the sincere affection of those who were intimately associated with him, and the respectful esteem of all.

This sketch would be incomplete without the addition of a few words concerning the home life of Dr. Allyn. Every man displays the qualities of his manhood in the family circle and home environment. Selfishness, ill temper and a despotic spirit were unknown at his fireside. He was the king and high priest of his household, yet ever patient, kind, forbearing and affectionate. He was married at the age of twenty-four to Miss Emeline Huntington Denison, who died in 1844, leaving two small children, Charles and Emma, bereft of a mother's care. He afterwards married Miss Mary Buddington, who adorned his home and shared his honors for many years. She was the mother of three children, Joseph, Ella, and Hattie, of whom the first two are still living. Mrs. Allyn was a woman of refinement, and presided over the home with dignity and grace. She aided very materially in maintaining the high social position of her husband. The oldest daughter, Emma, after teaching several years in Illinois Female College at Jacksonville, married Mr. William Hypes, of Lebanon, and went back to the old home to live; so, at the death of Mrs. Allyn, October 20, 1879, the management and cares of the household fell upon the capable shoulders of her daughter Ella, who proved a gracious hostess, and nobly did the honors of her father's home. Four years after the death of Mrs. Allyn another great sorrow shadowed his heart, when the sickle of the grim reaper touched the youngest of the family, his lovely daughter Hattie, and this fair, sweet flower was removed from his home to bloom in the gardens above.

"Oh, not in cruelty, not in wrath
The reaper came that day;
'Twas an angel visited the green earth
And took the flower away."

After a little more than a year of rest from anxious toil and corroding care this venerable schoolmaster, surrounded by loving family and friends, and with honors thick upon him, passed to his eternal rest and final reward. "God's finger touched him, and he slept." His name will ever shed a halo around the university over which he presided so efficiently and so long. The Alumni will ever cherish his memory and hold in reverence the name of Robert Allyn, the beloved father of this institution.

"To live in hearts we leave behind
Is not to die."

**LIBRARY
OF THE
UNIVERSITY OF ILLINOIS**

JOHN HULL.

JOHN HULL, A. M.

Professor John Hull, the second President of the Southern Illinois State Normal University, was born in Marion county, Illinois, February 6, 1839. The home of his parents was near Salem, not far from the homestead of the parents of Colonel William Jennings Bryan. He was fortunate in the fact that kind providence saw fit to place him, in the beginning of his career, in one of the strongest counties, educationally, in Illinois; a county which has furnished more students to, which has had more graduates to its credit, and has taken more honors in the Southern Illinois State Normal University than any other county, save Jackson. Here, in a log school house with the then usual puncheon benches, and the stern, spectacled "master," with his rule, hickory switch and ink-horn, John Hull learned the elements of education and laid deep and firm the foundation for an honored an influential career.

In 1857 he entered the State Normal School in Normal, Ill., and with characteristic thoroughness and industry mastered the course in three years, graduating with honors. He was immediately made principal of the Salem, Ill., public schools, and such was his success, even at his old home, that he was called to a place as teacher of mathematics in the Illinois State Normal, which chair he filled with eminent satisfaction until 1865, when the Bloomington schools were placed in his charge. Although he was then but twenty-three years of age, he managed them for two years with signal success. Recognizing his unusual ability, Brewer & Tiliston, then one of the largest publishing houses in the country, offered him the general western agency for their publications. While his preference was for school work proper, the large increase in salary tempted him to abandon his profession for a time. But the citizens of Bloomington were not content to leave him entirely out of the management of their schools, and he was elected a member of the Board of Education of that city, in which capacity he served four years, years marked by notable improvement in the even then excellent system of schools there.

In 1868 he founded "The Schoolmaster," afterward "The Chicago Schoolmaster" and still later "The Illinois Schoolmaster." Through this recognized authority on the theory and practice of teaching Professor Hull became known throughout the country. Here he was trained in that terse, accurate, comprehensive style which made his educational epigrams so much quoted and which has made him so much sought as a writer on educational subjects throughout the country in the educational press. It was during this time, 1869-1875, that he was County Superintendent of Schools of McLean County, the largest and richest county, other than Cook, in the state. By a close study of the practical needs of the public schools under his charge, he not only put McLean County in the front rank, educationally, but gathered a vast deal of experience and practical ideas, which have been invaluable to the hundreds of teachers who have gone out into the public schools of the state from the normal training system which he organized and direct supervision of which he retained as long as connected with this institution.

It was in 1875 Professor Hull was elected to a chair in the Southern Illinois State Normal University. He was immediately recognized as one of the strongest members of the faculty, and so thorough was his work, and so patent his ability in all lines of school work, that upon the resignation of Dr, Robert Allyn in 1892, after an extensive canvass of the country for a worthy successor to the honored and eminently successful retiring President, the Board of Trustees tendered the place to Prof. John Hull and he was inaugurated as regent. The exhibit of the Southern Illinois State Normal University at the World's Fair that year, prepared by Regent Hull, attracted the attention of the educational world, and brought the school into worldwide renown.

During all these years Professor Hull had been prominent in the educational societies of the state, and was always the personal friend and advisor of the succeeding State Superintendent of Public Instruction. Although not a politician in the usual sense of the word, and not ambitious for public office, he was several times prominently mentioned for the office of State Superintendent of Public Instruction, and although urged by his friends to allow his name to be used, he made no effort to secure the nomination. He was, in 1873 '74, chairman of the executive committee of the "County Superintendents' Association." He was also chairman of the executive committee of the "State Teachers' Association" in 1873, and was made president of this organization in 1874. In 1876 he received the degree of A. M., *pro merito*, from the Illinois Wesleyan University.

Professor Hull severed his connection with the Southern Illinois State Normal University in 1893, and took a place as president of the State Normal School at River Falls, Wisconsin. After serving this school for one year the condition of his health caused him to resign and he went into the Rocky Mountains. He is now editing a daily paper in New Whatcom, Washington.

HARVEY W. EVEREST, A. M., LL. D.

Few men have come into closer touch with the great body of people whose lives needed the uplift that comes from a great soul than has Dr. H. W. Everest.

Dr. Everest is a native New Yorker. He was born amid the rugged Adirondacks, in Sussex county, near the village of Hudson, May 10, 1831. Amid these characteristic highlands he spent his early youth, his parents having moved from New England. His lot was the common lot of all farmers' boys of that period and of that region.

The common schools of those days were *very* common. But such as they were they gave our friend, the good Doctor, an impulse which has kept him moving for more than half a century. At the age of sixteen he had progressed far enough with his studies to justify the authorities in placing him in charge of one of these schools. At the end of one term enough money had been saved to enable him to attend school at Crown Point on Lake Champlain. Here he spent one term. This was followed by another term in the teacher's calling, and at the age of eighteen he emigrated to Ohio. Here he lost no time in finding his way to the Geauga Seminary, a secondary school located at a place in Geauga county called Chester Cross Roads.

There was in attendance at this seminary another poor young man whose hard condition in the wilds of Ohio had begotten in him the determination to get out of life all there is in it for one who is willing to pay the price therefor. This young man was James Abram Garfield. Garfield and Everest were about the same age, and there soon sprang up a very strong attachment between them, which ripened into a brotherly love that grew stronger as

H. W. EVEREST.

**LIBRARY
OF THE
UNIVERSITY OF ILLINOIS**

the years went by till that dreary September day, 1881, when the martyr President breathed his last in the cottage by the sea.

Dr. Everest remained in the seminary but a few terms; from there he came to Illinois and taught school near the present city of Rock Island.

In the spring of 1853 we find him in attendance upon Hiram College, in Northeastern Ohio, where he remained two years. Being in need of funds he now opened a select school. When the term was finished he took charge of a church at Rome, Ashtabula county. From early life he had drunk deeply at the fountain of religious truth. His philosophy of man's religious duty is very simple, and he was able always to come near to any one who needed sympathy and help in his religious life.

It was while serving the church at Rome that he was selected by the Christian church as a suitable person to to receive a collegiate and Biblical education from a fund accruing from the sale of song books published by Alexander Campbell, of Bethany College, West Virginia. He repaired to Bethany College in due season and entered upon his duties as a student. This was in the dark days of the '50's, and it was not long before he found that his anti-slavery views were not acceptable to the management of the school. He and nine other Northern students were threatened by a pro-slavery mob, and feeling that very little genuine religious growth could come out of such conditions, he returned to Hiram College as teacher of natural science.

Here he remained studying and teaching till the summer of '60. During these years as a teacher and student in Hiram he was intimately associated with Garfield, who was president of the school. In the year of 1860 he entered Oberlin College in the senior year. He had previously married a Miss Sarah A. Harrison, of Painesville, Ohio. In the summer of 1861 he graduated from Oberlin in the classical course. War had broken out in the early part of '61, and Garfield felt that his country's call should be answered, and so he resigned the presidency of Hiram.

Upon the resignation of Garfield Dr. Everest was chosen as president. He remained at the head of this school from '61 to '64. During this time Garfield was seeing a good deal of actual service, and being an excellent scholar and skilled in the art of composition, he would weekly write his experiences and observations to the school. The letters were read from the platform before the assembled school, and were of no little interest.

Dr. Everest resigned the presidency of Hiram in 1864 to accept the presidency of Eureka College in Illinois. . Here he remained for eight years. The school greatly prospered under his charge, and many a preacher, teacher, or other professional man in Northern Illinois, recalls his school-days under Dr. Everest in Eureka.

In 1872 he resigned the presidency of Eureka and accepted the charge of the Christian church in Springfield, Ill. After two years here as pastor of the church he was called to a chair in Kentucky University, Lexington, Ky. Here he remained two years and returned to Illinois and took up the pastorate of the Christian church at Normal. At the end of one year as pastor of the church at Normal he was called to the presidency of Eureka, where he served five years. He was, therefore, president of Eureka College thirteen years in all.

In 1881 we find him president of Butler University, Indiana, where he remained six years. While here he received a call to the presidency of Garfield University, Wichita, Kansas. This was the most flattering educational field in which Dr. Everest had ever labored. A magnificent building had been erected. The field of work was uncontested, and for the first few years everything promised wonderful results. Through criminally bad management of the finances by the accredited financial agent, accompanied by an unparalleled collapse in real estate values throughout the entire west, the school was forced to scale down its expenses and finally was compelled to close its doors. Dr. Everest struggled manfully to keep the school on its feet, but having no moneyed interest to call upon, he was forced to yield to the inevitable.

Dr. Everest then took charge of the Christian church in Hutchison, Kas., where he was serving, when in the spring of '93 the Board of Trustees of the Southern Illinois Normal University selected him from among a score or more applicants for the presidency of that institution. He took up the duties of the office in September, 1893, and for four years he directed with rare tact and good judgment the interests of the school.

Dr. Everest entered upon his duties by a ready response to the calls from County Superintendents and city Principals to lecture to popular audiences. He had the power to take the simplest subject and make of it a most attractive one. He had unusual ability to reach conclusions from given premises. He took great delight in discussing the theory of the evolution of the material universe. He was also fond of discussing scientific questions, especially those relating to astronomy and physics: While holding the position of President of the Normal University he preached many powerful orthodox sermons.

He divided his time among all the Protestant churches known in Southern Illinois. He was not narrow, but was in the best sense of that word "broadguaged."

During the four years in which Dr. Everest directed the school there was a steady movement of the school toward its true end. A very elegant new building fitted for a library, gynasium, museum, and physical and chemical labratories was built; and in many ways the school became better known to the people of Egypt as the best and only place in which the young persons of this region may fit themselves for the noble profession of teaching.

At the end of four years because of ill health he severed his connection with the school and took the position of Dean of the Bible College in Drake University, where he now is. He is still in feeble health, but thinks there are indications of improvement.

Dr. Everest did considerable writing while at the head of the Normal. His little book, "The New Education," is a sparkling little volume. He also began while in the Normal another book since published—"The Science and Pedogy of Ethics." Several years ago he published "The Divine Demonstration."

The foregoing is a brief sketch of the life of a man who has been unusually active in doing for others. He is a man of broad culture, noble purposes, and definite aims. He holds malice toward none and has charity for all. May he live long and prosper is the wish of a host of very warm friends in Egypt.

D. B. PARKINSON, Ph. D.

"There is nothing more kingly than kindness,
There is nothing more royal than truth."

These words can be said of no one more truly than

D. B. PARKINSON.

**LIBRARY
OF THE
UNIVERSITY OF ILLINOIS**

of Dr. Daniel B. Parkinson, who has shown himself to be royal in truth and kindness.

He was born September 18, 1845, on a farm near Highland, Ill. His father is a prominent farmer of Madison county, and is still living on the old home place, purchased in 1844. Like the majority of farmers' sons, his summers were spent in work on the farm, and in them he seems to have inhaled in the winds of the prairies the love of nature and of nature's God.

During the winters he walked two miles to attend the little district school, where his sunny smile was welcomed by all, and on the play-ground could be heard his hearty laugh, and although full of boyish fun, he betrayed an earnestness in his work and a love of the just and right which has been one of the marked characteristics in his later life.

When he was eighteen his desire for greater knowledge than could be obtained in the little home school was so strong that his parents sent him to McKendree College, Lebanon, Ill., where he first came under the influence of our beloved Dr. Robert Allyn, who was at that time president of the college.

Then was formed a very dear friendship between teacher and pupil that was always strong.

Dr. Parkinson attended the college only during the winter terms for several years. It was during his first year he professed Christianity, and he has since '74 been an active member of the M. E. church of Carbondale.

In the winter of '65 and '66 he taught his first school in the rural district near home. He experienced all the gladness and sorrows of long walks and hard work, but from early childhood the art of looking on the "bright side" had been cultivated, so amid the hardships he found the goodness and gladness and retained the "inward sunshine, outward joy," so essential to the good teacher, but through it all there was the longing for higher work, and he entered McKendree again and graduated in the class of '68.

The following year he was principal of the Carmi public schools. His interest in natural sciences growing all the time, the next autumn he was elected to the chair of mathematics and natural sciences in Jennings Seminary, Aurora, Ill., where his tact and dealing with young men and young women was very noticeable. So successful was he here that he remained for three years, when his love of learning again compelled him to seek for greater knowledge, and he entered the Northwestern University at Evanston, Ill., doing special work in physics and chemistry. On July 1, 1874, so proficient had he become in these branches that he was offered the chair of natural philosophy and chemistry in the Southern Illinois Normal University, then about to be opened, which he accepted. In addition to this work he has taught geology and astronomy. The love of learning he himself has he arouses in his students.

The wonders he showed us of the earth, the air, or the heavens, we always felt, through his instructions, were but the wonders that God had placed upon and around the earth for the use of man and the uplifting of His kingdom.

The trips to the coal mines for the study of the layers of coal, the rainbows upon the wall, the searching out of the stars, were all earnestness with the beauty and glory to enhance the hard tasks.

In 1874 McKendree College conferred upon Dr. Parkinson the title of Master of Arts.

On the 28th day of December, 1876, he was married to Miss Julia F. Mason, who had resigned her position of model school teacher the previous term. The following summer, in company with his wife, he conducted a Teachers' Institute among the Cherokee Indians, near Talequah, Indian Territory. His experience among the Indians was new and interesting, with his love of nature he soon brought out the fact that they, with wonderful skill, were able to draw any color the objects taught them. In the summer of '79, his wife's health failing, he took her West, where she died August 6th in San Jose, Cal., leaving a boy of one year and eight months to be cared for.

In '75 Dr. Parkinson was appointed by the Superintendent of Public Instruction of Illinois to examine candidates for state certificates.

With all of his other duties he has been active in the Y. M. C. A. work. It has been his custom to meet with the young men of the school for Bible study, and many young men away from home needing the advice of a true Christian man have been aided by the talks on duty. In July of '76 he was sent as a delegate to Toronto, Canada, to meet an international committee of the Young Men's Christian Association.

Dr. Parkinson on July 30, 1884, was married in Mt. Vernon, Ill., to Miss Alice Raymond, the art teacher of the University. Two children have blessed this reunion, Raymond and Alice.

For eighteen years he served as secretary of the faculty and his duties were not neglected for the Secretary's book of the faculty is a record well kept.

In '92 he was made Registrar of the Normal, a position he held for five years. In '96 he was made

President and in '97 McKendree again gave honors to her son, P. H. D. was added to his name. When in '98 it became necessary to fill the chair of President, vacated by Dr. Everest, nothing seemed more natural to the friends of Dr. Parkinson than that he should be offered the presidency.

Dr. Parkinson is filling the chair as president of the university with the same zeal and tact that he has exhibited during his remarkable career as a school man, and our university has long since taken rank as one of the leading schools of the day.

Entering the university as a young man, he has won his way into the hearts of thousands by the exercise of those qualities which have "made him a stimulating force among present, and a pleasant memory with past associates."

While, as students, we remember him as a man of energy, pleasantness, magnetism, firmness and earnestness, and yet through it all, and above all, we see in the wearing of his life, the golden threads of charity and courtesy, that charity that suffereth long and is kind, that courtesy which is

> "To do and say
> The kindest things in the kindest way."

And we, the Alumni of the S. I. S. N. U., trust that Dr. Parkinson may occupy the chair of president of our university long years to come, and may the sweet "peace that passeth all understanding" be with him.

**LIBRARY
OF THE
UNIVERSITY OF ILLINOIS**

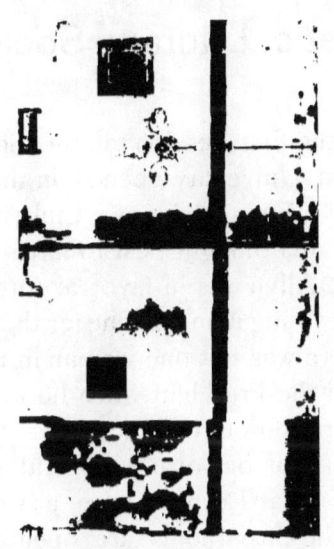

Zetetic Literary Society.

WHEN the first session of the Southern Illinois Normal University opened in the fall of 1874, a Young Men's Debating Club formed early in the term, but it was thought best to have a Literary Society also. Dr. Allyn was in favor of forming two societies; one for the young men and one for the young women. At this time there was but one woman in the faculty, and one student told the President when he was urging her to assist him in carrying out this plan that "when you give us girls teachers of our own sex, and separate class-rooms, I will do what I can to form a woman's society, but as long as the class-rooms are open to both sexes, with men as teachers, I will take no part in separating the social and literary life of the school." This idea prevailed in both faculty and school, and on this broad and liberal platform the first Literary Society of the Normal was founded. During the latter part of September a number of preliminary meetings were held, which were followed by a formal meeting in the northwest corner on the first floor of the Normal building the evening of October 9.

The minutes of the preliminary meetings give a clear idea of the founding of the Zetetic Literary Society:

On September 9 a petition was presented to the Board of Trustees and Faculty of the Southern Illinois Normal University praying for a hall and asking permission to organize a Literary Society in said university. The minutes show that R. H. Flannagan, one of the students, had received an answer to this petition, granting permission to the petitioners to organize a society for literary purposes.

Whereupon the following students assembled:

Robert H. Flannagan.   L. M. Kane.
John Qualls.   J. N. Law.
J. M. Reeder.   S. A. Maxwell.
Heber Robarts.   Mary Wright.
D. G. Thompson.   J. M. Osborne.
N. Ellen Sherman.   J. R. Dean.
C. E. Evans.   S. E. Spragg.

A committee was appointed to draft a constitution and by-laws, and they adjourned to meet in one week. They met at the appointed place and time and completed the organization of a society by adopting the constitution and by-laws as presented, and so became an integral part of the Normal work. They then proceeded to elect officers, as follows: Miss May Wright, President; Mr. Heber Robarts, Vice President; and Miss N. E. Sherman, Secretary. The President, on taking the chair and being called on for a speech, said: "It is evident why the ladies were given the important offices. It is well known that women are proverbial talkers, so we were put into positions to force us to keep still and allow you to do the talking. We will see that full justice is done you on all occasions."

They bravely began work in the bare, carpetless room, with no chairs, no tables, no curtains and no lights but a borrowed lamp, and a school-room bench served for seating. The President has said there were many laughable things connected with the hardships of those days. At that time there were no lights in the halls, or brackets arranged to hold them, and those of us who came without lanterns felt our way through the halls and up two flights of stairs, being certain of one thing—there was a light at the top, and this thought suggested many a quick idea and conception of the benefit of climbing to the light.

The needs of the society were great, and many articles of furniture had to be purchased before the society could make the room comfortable, but Dr. Allyn gave liberally, and they were greatly encouraged by the help received from an entertainment given by Professor Brownlee.

They had to begin at the beginning and work up by degrees, as there were many things to be learned by them before they felt that they understood the rules governing organized societies, which they were anxious to learn thoroughly. The energy and enthusiasm of the founders of this society were not to be overcome by difficulties and discouragements, but they pushed forward, met the hardships bravely, overcame them, and so placed the society on a firm foundation.

In a few weeks after organization they were able to purchase two chairs, about a dozen recitation benches, kerosene lamps, and a small stand which was used by both President and Secretary for several meetings. A committee was appointed to select names, which they submitted to the society in the next regular meeting. After due consideration and discussion the name Zetetic was chosen as a title, meaning "To seek;" also "Lovers of Knowledge." In the debate preceding this choice one excited speaker, urging the claims of the name Zetetic, emphatically exclaimed, "You know we are all seeking knowledge of lovers!" This blunder was followed by an uproarous shout of laughter that echoed and re-echoed unchecked from the bare walls.

The first program consisted of a declaration, an essay, and a debate. The President decided the debate, which was the custom in the society for many years. Shortly after the beginning of the society the faculty were elected as honorary members, also later, the Board of Trustees, the Governor of Illinois and John A. Logan. A library was started in a few weeks after organization to which the faculty donated a number of volumes, which were kept in the Normal Library until it was destroyed by fire in the year 1883.

As the first year drew to a close the subject of the spring entertainment was introduced. The first one given consisted of the usual recitations and essays, besides tableaux, an original dialogue and a Zetetic journal. The spring entertainment is a feature of the society work that has continued throughout the years and at the present time forms one of the most attractive events of commencement week.

The first president has told us the motto of our society was a chance thought. We were to have an open meeting and our hall was so bare we made in evergreen letters the motto, now our society watchword, and placed the words, "Learn to Labor and to Wait" around the window back of the platform. These words were left in the hall until they seemed a part of the society, so were adopted as its watchword.

Three years after organization an organ was purchased for the hall, which was replaced by a piano in the fall of 1880.

On October 9, 1877, Roberts' Rules of Order were adopted for use, which are still retained as authority.

On the morning of November 26, 1883, the society was in a prosperous condition, the floor was carpeted, the alcove curtained, on the walls were a number of choice pictures, a piano occupied one corner, the hall was comfortably seated and contained a large chair and stand for the President and a Secretary's table. It was a beautiful room of which the society justly felt proud, but that afternoon word was passed from room to room that the building was on fire. The first thought of many of the members was of the society hall, and through their efforts the furniture was carried out and most of it saved in good condition. In the late afternoon a called meeting of the Zetetic Society was held in the northern part of the campus, in which they voted to hold a meeting the next afternoon in Mr. Dunaway's parlor. At this meeting of November 27, a committee was appointed to find a suitable room in which to store the furniture saved from the fire, also a committee was appointed to find a room in which the society could hold its regular meetings until the normal could again be ready for occupancy. An office room on the west side of the city square was secured, in which the meetings were held until the following March, when the temporary normal was completed and the society was given the large recitation room in the south wing, which it occupied until the completion of the present building. It was then given for its permanent home the large, beautiful room in the northeast corner of the third floor, which it has beautified and made home-like and attractive in every way possible and which affords one of the best means of culture, disclipline and instruction in literary work and parliamentary business for the energetic, inquiring students who are ready and anxious to improve their opportunities.

This society started its career twenty-five years ago in a bare room, with no money in its treasury and no furniture, worked earnestly along through the passing years, meeting difficulties and discouragements bravely, and accomplishing all it could for the good of the students enrolled with it. During these years it has enrolled over one thousand members, and reaches the quarter centennial mark with a term enrollment of seventy-one active, working members, who are enjoying the fruits of the hard work done by the founders of the society, and who are striving to keep bright the honor due them and the organization they effected.

LIBRARY
OF THE
UNIVERSITY OF ILLINOIS

Socratic Literary Society.

IT was early in the spring term of the year 1875, if my memory serves me right, that seventeen or eighteen young men, then students of the Normal, formed the plan of a literary society. All of them were from the country, and had been engaged, more or less, in debating societies and the "Literary" of the rural school districts. They were, however, backward about displaying their literary and oratorical abilities, and, up to that time, had hesitated about appearing publicly in such capacities at the Normal.

After a number of meetings a committee was appointed to interview the faculty, and, with many misgivings, proceeded on their errand. The faculty, viewing the matter with very little concern, and not, at that time, recognizing the society work as a feature of the school, as it is now considered, thought it sufficient to allow the use of a large, bare room in the fourth or Mansard story of the old building. The old minute book, subsequently destroyed by fire, recited that a lamp was borrowed from Mrs. Joseph Warder for the first meeting. The only furniture provided was three or four recitation seats.

The members met together in the following week, and, from the small fund provided by membership fees, bought the material, and, with their own hands, constructed a platform; then chairs were purchased from the same fund, and, later, a hand-lamp and chandelier were procured.

There was a feeling of entire independence on the

part of the membership from school control that might have led (but, I am glad to say, never did,) to a violation of or breaking away from the school restraint.

The debates were a strong feature, and at each meeting of the society, in addition to the regular program, every member was entitled to be heard under the head of general debate. There was no time limit on speeches, and the hour of adjournment was not fixed by the faculty, or by any rules of the society. Often our adjournment hour was reached only with midnight, and after every member, possibly, had made one or more speeches, either in debate or under the head of business.

The business meetings were seriously conducted. Momentous questions arose. Oftentimes it was only by the firm rule of a master hand in the chair that personal altercations were avoided, but while this is true, the body never became so turbulent as some other deliberative assemblies I have seen.

As originally organized, the membership of the society was limited to the masculine class of students, but before a year had passed the question arose of amending the constitution so that the feminine side of the school might be admitted. Then arose discussions that were earnest and prolonged. A strong minority of the members of the society opposed the admission of the girls. All the various phases of the woman question were learnedly discussed by the boys. The future of the society, in case it should be turned over to the inroads of the fair sex, was depicted in darkest colors. Two-thirds of the members present at a meeting were necessary in order to amend the constitution, and two weeks' notice was required to be given of the time when the vote would be had.

A number of times the question was voted on, and lacked, perhaps, one or two votes of the necessary two-thirds. The final discussion and vote, however, took place on a night memorable to many of the old citizens of Carbondale, when a large railroad circus visited the city, and, in addition, torrents of rain fell. There were present at the meeting of the society six members, and after all had talked themselves hoarse a vote was taken, and, by a majority of four to two, the ladies were admitted.

The growth of the society had been slow prior to that event, but to the credit of the ladies be it said, they immediately took advantage of the opportunity, and in a short time the membership was doubled. Their influence was beneficial. The business was proceeded with more smoothly; the literary work was really of a higher grade, and a greater number of visitors were seen. As a result of the admission of the ladies a few of our members left us, but the remainder were always satisfied that the society only gained by their loss.

Some money had accumulated, and a carpet for the platform was procured. A motto must be had, and, after a great deal of labor, one was decided upon, which, I am sorry to say, contained so much bad Latin that it has since had to be reconstructed.

And how our interest centered around the elections; what earnest "button-holing" was done. With what force would we argue the advantage of our particular candidate. Looking back, it seems now that the events of the society were as real, were participated in with as much anxiety and earnestness, even more, than the regular work of the school.

There was a feeling that existed for some time, that

the faculty viewed the Socratic Society with suspicion, but looking back on the matter from this distance, I feel assured that the best wishes of this body, individually and collectively, were with the Socratic Society. I feel that they recognized that any attempt to patronize the society would have been detrimental, and it was probably as well that we were allowed to work out our own ends in our own way.

We learned many things there. Not alone that which we gathered from the text-books, but we gained some idea of that wider range of learning—of women and of the forces that control them. Along with the high ideals there formed, the great desire for knowledge, there was much of the practical—the application of what was learned. There was the strong ambition to succeed in whatever was undertaken, and we had a desire, not alone for the knowledge, and the ability that it would bring, but for the power it would give the individual as a member of society.

We sought leadership; we worked for it. At the beginning of a new term there was always the seeking out of good material; the contest with the opposite society to get the best members, to make the greatest additions in point of ability. Here, again, was an opportunity to apply the knowledge we were gaining of men and women.

The Socratic Society was founded on the broad principle enunciated in that most famous document, the Declaration of Independence, "that all men are free and equal," and while in the domain of knowledge, this may have qualifications, there should be no qualification of that right as applied to an opportunity to be given every individual to acquire knowledge. One of the fundamental principles of the society was its absolute democracy, and by that I mean nothing political, but that each member was considered the equal of every other; that in the domain of the work of the society no such a thing as an aristocracy existed. Especially did the society in its early years seek to help the members from the country. Oftentimes these were timid, and while having talent, were slow to assert themselves. The members of the Socratic Society, in its early days, were helpful to all such.

It was, probably, not until the year 1877 that the finances of the society were in such a condition that the question of procuring a piano might be considered. An organ had been purchased, and I well remember with what elation we added the office of organist to the list of officers to be elected. But the society, able to meet matters as they should arise, now decided that nothing less than a piano would do, and, by going in debt quite heavily, this acquisition was made. There was no thought of applying to the faculty, because, even with the trustees, in those days, finances were an item, and they would never have dared to put in a demand for appropriations an item for a piano for the literary society. But the piano was paid for, though it took the savings of several years to liquidate the indebtedness. Sad to say, this piano was burned when the old building was destroyed, and, with it, the archives of the society.

Many of the old members would delight to-day to turn the pages of the minutes of the earlier meetings, and re-visit the scenes of those days; to fight again the old contests, and mingle with the members, and again to feel the strong, warm attachments that were formed among the members of the society, for the society work brought the students nearer together, and they became more intimate than was possible in any other part of the school work.

In the early days the society contests were fought with an earnestness that almost amounted to bitterness. For weeks before, the question of the comparative merits of the members of the different societies would be canvassed. Hopes would be raised; acrimonious conversations would be had between the members; for our rivals, the Zetetics, were always on the alert to pick up a good member, or say a word derogotary to the Socratics.

At that day it seemed to our members that our rivals at the other end of the building always sat themselves upon a pedestal, looking down with calm condescension upon the Socratics. This treatment always had the effect of arousing the Socratics; and the further claim that the Zetetics were especially favored by the faculty was made, and, while it rankled, was universally met with derision by our members.

Up to the time of the new building, the Socratic Society obtained but slight recognition from the governing bodies of the school, and, in fact, the same might be said of the Zetetic Society; and it is to the credit of these organizations that by earnest work they forced themselves upon the faculty and trustees as necessary features of the school work, so that in the new building good halls, well furnished, were provided for them.

The old members took a pride in the literary society. and that pride is not lessened to-day, when, looking back over the years, we come to the conclusion that the work done in the society, when well done, is as invaluable to the student as any part of the school work. I am glad to know that the Socratic Society to-day is carrying forward the work so begun, and that in a large measure the same principles are found existing there, as at the foundation.

LIBRARY
OF THE
UNIVERSITY OF ILLINOIS

NORMAL HALL

Life's Awakening.

1874-1899.

I.

Eastward creep the mighty shadows
   Of the century's waning years,
Westward burns the sunset glory
   And the evening star appears.

Great has been the closing era—
   New-found wonders crowding fast,
Each swift year its truth or treasure
   Richer, rarer than the last.

Yet these late, resplendent ages
   Well may heed the lesson old:
Life is not in fame or pleasure,
   Learning's lore or hoard of gold.

Faith to kindle zeal heroic,
   Love to make the heart beat true,
Hope, still strong in doubt or sorrow,
   Shine like stars the ages through.

Man's own bosom is an empire
   Where his noblest deeds are done;
In the spirit's silent conflicts
   Are our truest victories won.

Rightly ruling, knowing, using
   Passions, longings of the heart,
Blending all in noble living—
   This is wisdom's highest art.

II.

When of old the weary shepherd
　Slept on Bethel's stony hight,
Angels o'er him kept their vigils,
　Wondrous visions filled the night.

To his couch celestial spirits
　Came to cheer him and defend,
And God's faithful promise given,
　Blessed him to the journey's end.

Paling star and glaring daylight
　Left him still that splendid hour;
All his later years and struggles
　Felt its animating power·

Still we sleep, on rocky pillows,
　In the clouded land of dreams,
Till our heavy eyes are smitten
　By some vision's thrilling gleams.

Then we look, with eyes annointed,
　On a new world fair and good,
Grasp the power, read the meaning
　Hid in truth misunderstood.

Heart and purpose are transfigured,
　All the place is holy ground;
Lowly gifts and humble objects
　With high worth and use are crowned.

III.

God still sends us inspirations—
　Still His patient angels stand,
Till our slow eyes are awakened
　And we see our Promised Land.

Here hath been our "Mount of Vision"
　For these five and twenty years;
Here hath wisdom's precious promise
　Taught us faith and calmed our fears.

In these halls have souls been quickened,
   Deeper, kinder motives stirred,
Hearts have pondered truth's ideals,
   Life's diviner music heard.

With us still abide these forces,
   Vital, helpful, never lost,
Potent still for strong endeavor
   When the soul is tempest-tossed.

Through thy life, these changing seasons,
   Many lives are true and strong,
Girded for heroic striving
   To withstand and vanquish wrong.

IV.

May thy beauty, Alma Mater,
   Glow and brighten as the dawn;
May thy gracious worth and wisdom
   Still from right and truth be drawn.

May thy light and benediction
   Long attend the coming age,
As thy fair name now is honored
   On the closing cycle's page.

May thy consecrated powers
   Still inspire and guide our youth
In the realms of highest virtue,
   In the love of God and truth.

Our Alumni Dead.

EVERY class that completes a course of study is bound together by common interests; and the ties of association are too strong for the daily petty rivalries to sever them. The friendships formed in this fellowship bind its members more closely as the day of separation comes, and each enters into the active work of the great, busy world, for which these years of preparation have fitted them. Joining and becoming part of the Alumni Association develops a general will out of this personal element, which rejoices in the successes of all its members, or follows the luckless ones with brotherly compassion, that centers the regard for the Alma Mater into a broader fellowship which recognizes the value of individual influence in whatever walk of life it is exercised; whether in the school-room, the home, the professions, or on a farm, personal character makes or mars the individual man or woman. Annually the circle widens, and the hearty greetings of the old-time friends makes welcome for the newer. But now and then we miss a well-known face, and a sense of loneliness steals into the rooms, while a longing for the cheery voice with the old ring of glad welcome fills the unbroken silence with memories of work well done, and of faithful, earnest endeavor. This memory brings its own healing in the promises of better things, and of life everlasting.

For the seventeen members of our Alumni who have finished their labors and been called to their reward, we have only tender, reverent words. We are better men and women for their having lived among us, and richer because of the inheritance they have left us of true thinking and noble living.

> "More homelike seems the vast unknown
>   Since they have entered there;
> To follow them were not so hard
>   Wherever they may fare;
> They cannot be where God is not
>   On any sea or shore:
> Whate'er betides, Thy love abides,
>   Our God forevermore!"

John C. HAWTHORN, of the class of 1876, was the first to go. He was born at Blair, Illinois, July 7, 1852. . He was of slender build and far from robust health, and his friends could not predict for him a long career. After completing the course in the Normal with the first class in 1876, he entered upon the study of law at Sparta, Illinois, and carried his work to a successful conclusion. After passing his examination and being admitted to the legal profession, he lived but few months to enjoy the fruits of his labors. He passed away November 15, 1880.

The class of '77 remain, and their records will be found among those who are bearing the "heat and burden of the day." The class of '78 has one representative in the spirit world—Charles E. Evans. He lived with his parents in Carbondale, and with a brother and two sisters entered the Normal the first year of its work. As a member of the Literary Society he showed a decided talent for oratory; this resulted, after two years' teaching in Randolph county following his graduation from the Normal, in his beginning the study of Theology at Evanston, Illinois. For several years he was a successful preacher in the Methodist Episcopal church, from which he was called home to his reward July 29, 1887.

The class of '79 consisted of but four members, and one early closed her labors.

Ida May McReery was born in Franklin County, Illinois, January 8, 1859, and died at Carbondale, Ill., October 10, 1881. From childhood she possessed a somewhat delicate constitution which never became rugged, while her intellectual powers were strong and vigorous. She was one of those persons in whom the intellectual held the supremacy over the physical. Yet she was the very embodiment of energy and made good use of the few years which were allotted to her. At the age of twelve she entered the M. E. church. Always cheerful, conscientious, courteous, faithful and consistent, she won the love and confidence of all who knew her. She graduated at the Southern Illinois Normal with the honors of her class in 1879. At the time of her death she was one of the teachers in the public schools of the city of Carbondale. Death found her at her chosen post of duty. Her death was peaceful and triumphant. Conscious almost until the last moment, her dying testimonies were such as to make Heaven seem very near and very real. Just before her spirit went home she sung distinctly, "I Am Trusting, Lord, in Thee."

So great were the love and respect for her among her acquaintances, that, after nearly a score of years have passed since her death, her name is still spoken softly and with reverence by all who knew her.

The next class to suffer by the "grim reaper" was that of '84. This class has the sad preeminence of having lost most heavily of all. On this roll stand the names of Fannie Aikman, May Duff, Carrie Ridenhour, and Maud Thomas.

Fannie A. Aikman was born at Marion, Ill., July 29, 1862; here she received her early training, entering the Southern Normal in 1880, she completed the course with the class of '84, and in the same month was married to D. L. Kimmell, a member of the Junior class. Mr. and Mrs. Kimmell passed two happy years at their home in Elkville; then disease of the lungs showed its presence. In spite of every effort of loving friends, assisted by all that skill could devise, she passed away April 13, 1887, at her home in Elkville. She was an earnest Christian, bowing calmly and trustingly to the Divine will. She felt the cheer of immortal sunlight. She left her husband, a little girl less than two years old, and hosts of friends to mourn their great loss.

May B. Duff was born in Benton, Franklin County, Illinois, January 6, 1864. In 1873 her parents came to Carbondale, which was ever afterward her home. Quick to learn and studious in her habits she spent the first year of her residence here in the public schools, and when but eleven years of age entered the model department of the Southern Illinois Normal University. With slight exception she remained in school constantly until her graduation with the class of '84. From early childhood she evinced religious tendencies, and from the time of her coming to Carbondale was a faithful attendant upon Sunday school instruction. In the summer of 1880 she was received into the fellowship of the Baptist church. The four brief years of her religious profession were marked by singular devotion and consecration. For some time a teacher in the Sunday school, it was her happy privilege to witness the profession of religion by nearly all her class. She thus proved herself to be a winner of souls. As a companion and friend, she was considerate of others, never intentionally wounding the feelings of those with whom she came in contact. To her parents she was ever faithful and true. Their wish was her delight. True to the energy of her temperment, she entered upon her work of teaching the next fall term. But a few weeks had passed when she was seized with what proved to be a fatal illness, Surrounded by her family and served with every attention, she gradually weakened, and on the morning of Tuesday, November 11, 1884, she entered the land where shadows never come.

Carrie Ridenhower was born in Johnson County on a farm, January 31, 1857. She was a successful teacher before entering the Normal, where she proved a good student, a pleasant acquaintance and a true friend. After graduation in 1884 she re-entered the profession of teaching in her native county, where with fresh vigor and interest she taught for four years. She married J. L. Mount, of Goreville, Illinois, and from a happy home was called away to the joy and rest of the faithful, in the fall of 1888.

Maude Thomas was born April 2, 1862, in the parish of Baglan, South Wales. She came to the United States with her family in 1870. For ten years her home was in Carbondale. During this period she completed the course of study at the Normal, graduating with an excellent standing in the class of '84. She taught two years in Cobden, Illinois, where she made many friends. From this school she went to Los Angeles, California, and, after a few months' work, was the victim of a fatal disease, and, returning to her home in Carbondale, passed quietly to rest on August 20, 1888.

Luella Hundley was born at Marion, Illinois, February 5, 1858. She was the oldest of four sisters, and when her parents died was still young; but she assumed the care of the three younger sisters, and while in school in the Normal kept house to make a place for them that all might be bound together by the family ties of a home. In her loving care and faithful devotion to duty she won the respect and admiration of her teachers and the sympathy and friendship of her school-mates. Ella, as she was known in school, was salutatorian of class of '86. She went to Texas the year following her graduation, and taught in the schools of Denton four years. She then returned to Illinois and taught at Kankakee and Harvard; after this she went to Arizona and taught at Prescott. Here she married H. T. Andrews, a lawyer of that place. She lost her life September 6, 1898, in her burning home at Prescott. With characteristic energy she re-entered the building to save some valuable papers. When half-way up the stairs the flames burst forth above and below. She perished before aid could reach her.

Edgar Stormant was born on a farm near Salem, Ill., January 7, 1865, he had unusual ability and while in school was remarkable for his thorough, scholarly work. Being of frail physique he decided after graduation in 1886 to go West for a few years. He was elected to the chair of science in the Territorial Normal at Tempe, Arizona. He married Mary A. Hill, class '87. After holding the chair of science two years he was elected to the presidency of the normal. In June of 1896 he resigned and returned to Illinois. He spent a year at the State University at Champaign and then took a position in the Streator High School. Here developed his deadly foe, consumption. Although he returned to Tempe in the summer of 1898 it was too late to arrest the disease. He passed away in a few months, surrounded by loving friends and attended by his faithful wife.

Carrie Blair was born near Sparta, Ill., August 2, 1862. She was a kind, loving daughter and sister. In early life she made a public profession of religion, joining the Reform Presbyterian church in Sparta. She took the full course at the Southern Normal, graduating therefrom in the class of '87, with the warm esteem of all who knew her. She taught ten years and was an eminently successful teacher, patient, persuasive and energetic. She taught in Collinsville, Ill., and Charleston, Ill. From the later place she went to Cedarville, O., where she filled the chair of mathematics in their denominational college, making warm friends outside her work, and winning the love and confidence of the faculty and students. While taking a mathematical course in Chautauqua University she was attacked by that dread destroyer, typhoid fever, from which she died September 2, 1895.

Kate E. Richards was born May 18, 1870, at Rockwood, Illinois, and entered the S. I. N. U. in the fall of 1885. She was a pretty, bright girl, a good student, and a loved companion. After graduating in the class of '88 she taught two years, and then was married to Mr. Steward, of Delphos, Kansas. Death soon entered the home and bore the young wife from the pleasures of earth to the joys of the better land.

Frank E. Trobaugh was a Jackson County boy, born September 11, 1868, and brought up on his father's farm. He entered the Normal and, after graduating with the class of '88, taught one year; then he began the study of medicine, completing his preparation with honor in Cincinnati in 1891. He married Miss Louisa Waller, who had been a fellow-student with him at the Normal, and began the practice of his profession at Murphysboro, Illinois. Every one knew and trusted Frank, and his practice rapidly grew. He has been called from ministering unto others into the rest prepared for the faithful.

Mabel E. Smith was born December 10, 1869, died

September 21, 1892. She completed the course of study in the public schools of Carbondale, Illinois, in the spring of 1887; entered the Southern Illinois Normal University the next fall, graduating in 1890. She early developed a talent for and love of music, receiving instruction from private teachers during her attendance at the public schools and Normal University, and, after graduating from the Normal, taking an extended course of instruction and voice culture in the musical conservatories of St.' Louis and Chicago. She devoted herself to teaching music for a time with encouraging success, but during August of 1892 she was stricken with typhoid fever, and after a continued illness of a month she passed away. Her obliging disposition made her ever ready to use her great talent for the good of others. Often at Alumni reunions memory brings back to Normal hall the thrilling music of her lovely voice.

Mary E. Hill was born at Centralia February 2, 1878, entered the Normal September 10, 1889, and graduated with the class of '91. After teaching four years she married Broughton T. Smith, of Equality, on June 24, 1896, and died October 23 of the same year. Thus, far too early, was our beloved and attractive friend called from those who loved her, on earth, to the bright mansions above.

Charles L. Stout was born February 5, 1866, at Chauncy, Ill., and entered the Normal, graduating with the class of '93, after which he returned to his work in Nashville, Ill., as principal of the high school, but in a few months he was called from his labors. He was a faithful teacher, and an earnest Christian, and won the respect and confidence of all. It was felt as a loss to the community that his work must cease so soon.

Eric Mohlenbrock was born at Campbell Hill, Ill.,

January 12, 1874, and entered the Normal January 5, 1891. He ranked high in his class, graduating in 1894. He was frail in body and was urged by his friends to go west for a while before beginning his chosen work of teaching. His ambition was too great to permit this, so he entered upon his profession in Flora, Ill., the following fall as Principal of the High School. So faithful and earnest was he that before spring his health failed under the strain of large classes and personal interest in the success of each student. He then reluctantly left his work and went west in search of health; but too late. He died in California in the summer of 1895. So good a mind and so pure a character fitted him for usefulness here, but equally fitted him for the joys of Heaven.

Bertram John Amon was born in Louisville, Ky., January 20, 1877. He came to Carbondale with his parents when but eight months old. In 1881 he moved to Chester, where he studied in the public schools until his return to Carbondale in 1893. He graduated from the Normal in 1897, and was Principal of the Crainville school the following school season. Bert, as he was familiarly known, was one of our best young men; kind, sociable, and in every way a good companion. His death was the result of this desire to make others happy. His sister, who was president, wished to take the children of the Junior League of the M. E. church on a picnic, so Bert went to help give them a good time. After dinner he went with the little boys for a swim. He first waded in, to be sure it was safe for the boys; he stepped into a hole, and was drowned before aid could reach him, June 29, 1898. Thus ended a life bright and joyous, and a cloud of sorrow settled down upon many hearts. Thus far Bert is the last to leave our fellowship below and become an alumnus from the school of the Great Teacher Himself.

**LIBRARY
OF THE
UNIVERSITY OF ILLINOIS**

PRESIDENT'S OFFICE.

Twenty-Fifth Anniversary.

SUNDAY, JUNE 11, 1899.

THE morning was pleasant, not too warm, and at the appointed time Normal Hall was well filled with strangers, townspeople and students, who came to hear Dr. Edwards, who was to preach the Baccalaureate sermon. At eleven o'clock the Faculty, Senior class and others, who had met by appointment in the office, marched to Normal Hall under the direction of Prof. S. E. Harwood, where the following program was given:

Anthem—"Send Out Thy Light,"..............................Choir
Invocation...Rev. H. H. Branch
Bass Solo—"Incline Thine Ear"........Prof. J. H. Brownlee and Choir
Reading of Scripture.................................Rev. J. W. Parkhill
Hymn—"Coronation"...................................Congregation
Prayer...Rev. C. B. Besse
Solo—"Babylon".....................................Miss Bessie Johnson
Baccalaureate Sermon....Rev. Richard Edwards, LL. D., Bloomington
Anthem—"Praise Ye the Father"...............................Choir
Announcements.......................................Prof. H. W. Shryock
Benediction...Rev. W. S. Errett

In introducing Dr. Edwards to the audience Dr. Parkinson spoke of him as being one who was present at the dedication of the first building, twenty-five years ago the 1st day of July, and as taking part in those exercises as one of the speakers. Dr. Edwards was at that time President of the Normal at Normal, then the only normal school in the state. He had since served one term as State Superintendent of Public Instruction. Several of the others who were present have passed away, among whom were mentioned Hon. T. S. Ridgeway, of Shawneetown, who was for eighteen years President of the Board of Trustees; Dr. James Robarts, of Carbondale, who was for twelve years secretary of the Board, and Dr. Robert Allyn, the President of the school till 1892. In response Dr. Edwards said that he was not only present at the dedication of the first building in 1874, but was present at the laying of the corner-stone in 1870. The Doctor said, further, that he could see the influence the school had exerted in the town and even in the audience now before him.

Dr. Edwards took his text for the Baccalaureate sermon from the nineteenth verse of the twenty-fifth chapter of Matthew: "After a time the lord of those servants cometh and reckoneth with them." The Scripture lesson that had been read from the same chapter brought out the fact that before going to a far country this lord of the servants had given to each an amount of money that he was to use during his lord's absence. Those who had used the portion intrusted to them wisely were commended, while the one who had indolently hidden his portion in the earth was condemned. The Doctor took as his theme the idea of responsibility. These servants were left free to do as they chose with that which was intrusted to them. But this freedom involved responsibility for how it was used. Does not all freedom involve responsibility? Opportunities are the talents that are given to us, and we will be held to an account for how we use them. The Scripture gives examples of those who have used the freedom given them. Paul was one of them who said: "I press forward to the mark of the high calling in Christ Jesus." In this he accepted the responsibility placed on him and did all he could to meet the expectations of his Lord and Master. Many others in modern times were spoken of as having followed in the same pathway.

A rudder of a ship is of no use unless it is used. So is the responsibility placed on a human being. It is in meeting these responsibilities in the right way that makes character and helps mankind.

Young people in these times have opportunities given them of acquiring an education. They are endowed with mental faculties and given the chance to use them. Was this for no end? No, it was for a purpose. Human faculties are the talents our Lord has left with us, and with us lies the responsibility of using these so that we may hear the "Well done, good and faithful servant." Never since time began have the avenues of learning been so numerous as now. There is inspiration in the thought. and vast numbers are availing themselves of these opportunities. This culture that may be acquired means the mastery of the mind that conduces to power.

Sometimes it occurs that a young man refuses to avail himself of the opportunities he has for improving his mind. You see such gathered in groups about places of resort, or amusement, or dissipation, where there is nothing suggestive or elevating, but everything tends to lead down instead of up to a better life.

Culture is an essential factor in the usefulness of man. The future will require larger knowledge than the past has required or the present is requiring. Sound scholarship is essential to the saving of the nation from the dangers that beset it.

If scholarship is good it must be good for something. Knowledge means a duty to the one possessing it. The scholar is responsible for the use of his knowledge. It should make men and women what they ought to be in the sight of God and man. Is it not true that the more one knows of God the more he reverences the source of this knowledge?

I know that all scholarship does not accomplish all the results I have spoken of—does not produce all the results. Such scholarship is but fragmentary. It is barren of desirable results because it is not complete in some of its essential parts.

Scholarship must subserve the necessities of the outward life. Without the utilization of science the universe is alien to man. Let scholarship help man to establish a helpful and right use of his surroundings.

But teach man to tell the truth. Are you ambitious to enter the field of politics? Find out what the real wants of mankind are. Look with scorn on what is only to promote temporary success.

The teacher's work leads him to look for results that are to be seen only in the future. The savage lives only from day to day. He hunts the animal whose flesh is to satisfy his present hunger and lies down in his wigwam contented and happy. Or if the result of the chase is not a success he endures the pangs of hunger with stoicism. The skin of the animal he eats goes to make a garment to cover his body, or to make a tent in which he may live, a shelter from the sun in summer and a meager protection from the cold of winter. But civilized man prepares for the future as well as for today. He does not depend on the uncertainties of the chase, but tills the ground that it may bring forth more abundantly and makes the earth and the forest contribute to the comforts of his home.

It is said that knowledge is power. Many forms of knowledge may be fragmentary and of but little use. But the knowledge we get from the right study of good books is of great worth. The thoughtful reader of good literature is in the best of company. Man puts his best thought into the book he publishes, and its reader is in the best of society.

In every field he may choose to enter the scholar may secure respect and power. The scholar is rising in public estimation. But with this added power comes added responsibility. What should be said of the man who had the power to better humanity and refused to use it? On the other hand what blessings are conferred on the man who has this power and does rightly use it?

"After a long time the Lord of those servants cometh and reckoneth with them." Shall we regard this as a threat? Away with such an idea! Let rather the thought be impressed that duty is an inspiration and not a burden. Let it be felt that the voice of duty is the voice of God.

In conclusion he said: "Members of the graduating class, you are today to take your leave of this institution. Can I say anything more inspiring than has already been said? Go forth and accept responsibility. Thank God for the opportunity to do something for humanity. The standards here are not so low that you have been able to float. You had to work for what you have secured. Thank God for this. When shown a responsibility as you go out into the world accept it in the sight of God. You have made a good beginning in an education. Continue in the way you have begun and the world will be blessed.

SUNDAY EVENING, JUNE 11.

In the evening the Normal Hall was again filled with those who came to listen to a program given under the auspices of the Young Men's and Young Women's Christian Associations. The program, as given and printed on sheets distributed at the door in the morning, was as follows:

Doxology..Congregation
Invocation..Rev. W. S. Errett
Song—"Faith is the Victory"................................Choir
Reading from Corinthians 12.....................Rev. H. H. Branch
Prayer..Rev. J. W. Parkhill
Anthem—"Lord of Heaven"...................................Choir
Address........................Rev. F. M. Hubbell, Belvidere, Ill
Anthem—"Oh, for a Thousand Tongues".......................Choir
Announcements................................Prof. S. E. Harwood
Benediction......................................Rev. C. B. Besse

In introducing Rev. Mr. Hubbell to the audience Dr. Parkinson spoke first of the organization of the Christian Association. Soon after the opening of the school in 1874 several of the young men, led by one of the professors, met for prayer in a room down town that had been used for a billiard hall. These early meetings were felt to be helpful to the students, and were soon transferred to a room in the Normal building. At first they had no connection with the college Christian Association, but later united themselves with the organization. As time passed it was thought best to divide the organization, and the Young Women's Christian Association was formed. In looking about for a speaker for this evening it was thought best to select one who had been identified with the association, and Rev. F. M. Hubbell, of Belvidere, Ill., who, as a young man was identified with the Young Men's Christian Association at about the middle of its history, was selected.

In response Mr. Hubbell said, in referring to his connection with the school eighteen years ago: "The fore-part of September, a green country boy, sixteen years old, might have been seen leading an old, red cow into town, when the cow was not leading him, which was much of the time. The cow was led down one of the back streets to a place where his father was moving that he might send the boy and his brother to the Normal. That boy was the present speaker, who had the pleasure of being a student in the Normal for two years, ending with the close of the spring term of 1883. It was only about a week ago that the invitation to address you was received, and under other circumstances it would have been refused. But with it came back the memories of those early days of my school-life in Carbondale, and I cheerfully accepted the invitation."

In speaking further of reminiscences of school life Mr. Hubbell said: "It seems to me there is something constitutionally wrong in any one who does not cherish fond memories of his school-life. It is this that brings together year after year the alumni of our colleges.

"Our schools should be a place for the recognition of the essential elements of human progress. They should be where we learn to know the social problems that confront us. Among those are the problems of the relation of labor and capital. Not that I would encourage the antagonisms between labor and capital that are often seen, but would leave the solution of this and other social problems to the schools to settle.

"In discussing these questions one essential element is usually left out of consideration, and that is the element of religion. As it is generally considered, only the selfish side of human nature, the ego, is taken into account. On this factor, it is said, rest our commercial relations. By this selfish spirit the weak are crushed by the strong, the rich are made richer and the poor are made poorer. Even the scientist in his biological researches finds this element constantly at work; the strong prey upon the weak, and life is maintained only 'by the survival of the fittest.' Nature hobbles, as it were, on one crutch, instead of walking on two legs. But the true student of social problems must also recognize altruism. During the progress of the evolution of the human race God has added to self-consciousness benevolence and other religious elements. In the higher development of civilization these are constantly crying out for recognition. It is this altruism that has not had its just recognition by science heretofore, but which is essential to the true development of scientific thought. The one who would solve the problems of our social system must recognize the religious side of human life.

"The student of philosophy admires the clear, philosophical insight of Bacon. But how little does Bacon seem when he learns of his private life and associations. The student of literature admires the brilliant thoughts and the elegant verse of Byron. But when he looks at the private life of Byron how little there is to admire in the man. So, too, the admirer of the writings of Voltaire, when he sees in history the private life of the writer, will be disgusted with the monstrosity developed out of such a system of false philosophy of life. The time is coming—yea, in a measure, now is—when one will look to the practices of those who are set up as leaders of society and thought. The world's great cry is for character, not for culture alone; for worth, not power.

"In conclusion, work out a philosophy of life based on the principles left us by the humble Nazerene nineteen centuries ago, and human society will move forward."

MONDAY MORNING, JUNE 12.

At ten o'clock the exercises of the first six grades of

the Practice School or Training Department were given in Normal Hall. The music, other than that which was part of the school exercises, was furnished by an orchestra from Olney, which had been secured to furnish music for the exercises of the week.

The program as prepared was a cantata—"Picnic Day"—by Charles H. Gabriel, arranged and adapted to the little folks by Miss Adda P. Wentz, who has charge of these six grades. The opening of the exercises was with a prayer by Dr. Richard Edwards, of Bloomington. The program as printed is as follows:

1. Prelude—"March".................Chorus marching as they sing
2. Recitation—"Spring Time"............................Quartermain
3. "Away, Away"..Chorus
4. "In the Tree Top," semi-chorus...........Grades Three and Four
5. "In Woodland Glen"-recitation and chorus..Grades Three and Four
6. Physical Exercises........................Third and Fourth Grades
7. "Expectations"—song and chorus.....................Primary Boys
8. "Ring Merry Bells"...................... Girls of Primary Grades
9. "The Storm"....................... Full Chorus of all the Grades
10. "Back to the Woods"—march and chorus................. By All
11. "What the Robin Said"—song....... Girls of Grades Five and Six
12. "Rondell"—exercises............... Girls of Grades Five and Six
13. "Now to the Woods"—song.......... Girls of Grades Five and Six
14. "Jolly Boys" .... Boys of Grades Five and Six
15. "Who's to Blame?"...............................Full Chorus of All
16. "Echo Song"...Full Chorus
17. "Sing and Swing"—waltz song...........Fifth and Sixth Grades
18. Recitation..Sixth Grade
19. "Sing on, Sweet Birds"—waltz song.........Grades Five and Six
20. "On the Way From School"..........................Full Chorus
21. "A Jolly Time"...........Full Chorus, marching out as they sing

There was no break in the program after it was once begun by the little folks, marching in singing till they marched out again in the same way. The whole performance was a unit, it might be said, but parts of a single piece. It was a fine model of what might be done under proper leadership by a company of children. As such it was probably the best program for the little folks that has been presented by the Training Department in the history of the school. A fitting quarter centennial exhibition of the work of the department.

MONDAY AFTERNOON, JUNE 12.

The exercises of the seventh and eighth grades were held in the afternoon, and after they were through there were some games by the Physical Culture Department on the campus east of the main building. The program was rendered as printed, as follows:

Prayer................................Prof. Samuel E. Harwood
Quartet—"School March"—Played by Misses Ethyle Reeves and
    Winona Etherton and Masters John Mitchell and Robert Teeter.
Recitation—"A Day in School".....................Percy Dickerman
Essay—"Domestic Habits of the Filipinos"..............Grace Storm
"Emmet's Lullaby"..Chorus
Quotation Drill—An exercise in giving quotations in concert when
    the author was named.
Recitation—"Patchwork Philosophy"....................Lucy Allen
Piano Solo..John Mitchell
Debate—*Resolved*, That it is better for a person to spend the first
    fifteen years of his life in the city than in the country. Affirmative, Donald Kirk. Negative.....................Grace Brandon
Quartet—"Awake Sweet Music's Gentle Strain"—Ethyle Reeves,
    Winona Etherton, John Mitchell and...............Robert Teeter
Paper—"The Lake"..............................Albert Thompson
Instrumental Duet—"Over the Waves"—Piano, Floyd Halstead;
    Mandolin......................................Bessie Halstead
Recitation—"Some Modern Public Schools"......Raymond Parkinson
Anniversary Chorus—Written by Alice Brush, of the 8th grade,
    and Ethyle Reeves, of the 7th grade.

At the beginning of the exercises Prof. Davis, who has charge of these two grades, announced that the work presented was almost exclusively the work of the pupils, the effort being to make them as early as possible independent workers. The parts were well committed and well rendered.

Prof. S. B. Whittington, who has charge of the physical training, was not present to conduct the exercises in the afternoon at the close of the entertainment by the 7th and 8th grades, nor will he be present at any of these exercises. A little more than a week ago his physician told him it was best that he should drop his work for the rest of the school year on account of sickness. But the work had been put into the hands of the captains of the different classes who were to play, and the work went on as originally planned. The first was a game of hurl ball, followed by pole vault, hurdle race and hammer throw. Much interest was manifested in these games, as was evinced by the large number who staid to witness them.

MONDAY EVENING, JUNE 12.

By 8 o'clock the hall was well filled by the audience that had assembled to witness the rendering of the program prepared by the Zetetic Literary Society. On the outside of the cover of the neat program that was received at the door was printed "1874–1899," the society dating its organization back to the first year of the opening of the school. The program was divided into two parts, a literary part and a rendering of one of Shakespeare's plays, as follows:

1. Music.......... .... **Miss Mertz**
2. Invocation......................... **Prof. Carlos E. Allen, A. B.**
3. President's Address...... ....**Willis Gerard Cisne**

The speaker said that this evening is given the twenty-fifth exhibition of the Zetetic Literary Society, and as a society we are proud of our record. The work of the society is important in the work of the school. Of the hundreds whose names have been enrolled on the society many are filling or have filled high positions of honor and of trust, while others are teachers exerting influences for good.

4. Recitation—"Daniel Pereton's Ride"............Kate F. Chandler

This was well rendered.

5. Vocal Solo—"The Heavenly Dream"...............H. W. Temple
6. Oration—"Reformation of our Industrial System"...J. I. McKnelly

The speaker pleads for a broader scholarship as one of the means of curing the evils of our industrial system.

7. Essay—"Off the Grand Banks".......................Mary Fryar

The theme of the essay was suggested by a picture in one of the art journals, in which an old sailor was the central figure.

8. Euphonium Solo....................................Walter Crow
9. Oration and Delivery of Diplomas—"New Responsibilities"..I. Victor Iles

The speaker touched upon the responsibilities of early nations, and compared them with those of the present day. As the responsibility of a nation is increased by increased advantages and education, so the responsibility of the individuals composing the nation increases. At the close of the oration Mr. Iles delivered the society diplomas to those of the Senior class who are members of the Zetetic Society.

10. "Much Ado About Nothing."

This was the second part of the program. Costumes befitting the play had been secured from Chicago, which, with appropriate stage scenery, made very necessary adjuncts for a successful rendering of the play. Each entered with spirit the character assigned him or her, and made the rendering of the play a decided success. The cast of characters was as follows:

Don Pedro.. ....A. J. Reef
Claudio..Roscoe Baker
Benedick...H. L. Freeland
Leonato.. ....Roy F. B. Davis
Antonio ....Thomas Hobbs
Dogberry..Harmon Etherton
Verges...Samuel Toler
Beatrice...Stella B. Dixon
Hero..Emma McLin
Ursula...Maude Williams
Convade..Thomas Bourland
Borachio..Robert Brown
Friar..J. T. Montgomery
Watchmen: { ....Wm. Brandon
              ....Gregg Garrison

TUESDAY, JUNE 13—10 A. M.

It was intended to give a game of basket ball in the gymnasium first and then repair to the campus for the rest of the games that had been provided for. But the heavy rain till time for the exercises to begin delayed the opening and made a change of program necessary. The games as played in the gymnasium were:

Basket Ball..By the Girls
    Misses Tanner and Marron, Captains
Basket Ball..By the Boys
    Messrs. Gambel and Boomer, Captains.
Valley Ball..By Both Boys and Girls

TUESDAY—2 P. M.

Quite an elaborate program had been prepared for this occasion and headed "Quarter Centennial Non-Graduate Exercises," to be given by members of the school at some time during the last twenty-five years, but who had not completed any of its courses of study. The program as rendered was quite different from the one printed, but was very interesting. Hon. L. M. Bradley, of Mound City, was president of the occasion. The following is the rendered program :

1. Music..Orchestra
2. Address...........................Hon. D. W. Helm, Metropolis

The theme upon which Mr. Helm spoke for a few minutes was, "What the World Needs and What the Normal Schools Are Doing to Supply That Need." Is it possible that nations must go through a period of rise to glory and then have their fall and pass away, or may they enjoy a perpetual existence? We prefer to hold to the later view. In order to attain this end we must not be controled by selfishness, but must work for the common good, both of the nation and humanity. The common school system is the most powerful agency in bringing about these ends, in uplifting the common people. The influence of the Southern Illinois Normal University has not been confined solely to the southern part of the state. There is not a county in the state but has felt its influence, and it has gone out into other states.

3. Vocal Solo..................Mrs. Dora Lee McCracken, Anna, Ill.

This was highly appreciated by the audience.

4. Addres.............................Mr. W. F. Bundy, Centralia

Mr. Bundy came into the school in 1879, and when he left at the close of the spring term of 1884 there were few he did not know intimately, and none he did not know by sight. As to the influence the school has in transforming a boy, he said: "If you had a good photograph of me as I entered the school, and one of me as I am now, it would be the best advertisement the school could have. Before coming here I had read of several funny men such as Bill Nye and Artemus Ward, but I thought

RECEPTION ROOM.

**LIBRARY
OF THE
UNIVERSITY OF ILLINOIS**

Professor Brownlee was the funniest of them all."

5. Violin Solo..........................Mr. P. E. North, Carbondale
6. Recitation—"A la Del Sarte and Bello"..Blanche Keeney, Chicago

This was so well received by the audience that Miss Keeney was called out again, when she gave a rendering of "Bertie McCarty." Miss Keeney was here when the school passed through the ordeal of fire, since which time she had graduated from the School of Oratory of Chicago.

7. Piano Solo...................Miss Dora Louise Mertz, Carbondale
8. Address......................Rev. F. M. Hubbell, Belvidere, Ill

Mr. Hubbell made a good talk, the point made being that a greater influence is exerted by the non-graduates of the school than by the graduates, because they are so much more numerous—about twenty to one. As a rule they stay here long enough to catch the spirit of the school, and then go out to graduate from some other special school, or; with new aspirations, go to work as teachers in the common schools.

9. Music..Orchestra
10. Prof. Brownlee read an interesting letter from Charles G. Neely, of Chicago, now Circuit Judge of Cook County.
11. Trio—Piano and Mandolin...A.G. Purdy, Fred Wykes, Rex Burnett
12. Here Prof. Brownlee read a letter from Mr. Fred Merrills, of Belleville.
13. Another letter was read by Prof. Brownlee from Hon. A. G. Abney, of Harrisburg, Ill. All the writers of these letters expressed regret that they could not be present at Carbondale this jubilee week.

Music..Orchestra

TUESDAY EVENING, JUNE 13, 8 O'CLOCK P. M.

Last evening the hall was well filled at the time for opening, perhaps more so than on Monday evening, as more strangers were in town. The program of this evening was given by the Socratic Society, and was as follows:

1. Grand March......................'.......................Orchestra
2. Invocation. ....Samuel E. Harwood, M. A
3. Address by the President..................W. Gordon Murphy

Mr. Murphy spoke of the aims of the society in its work in the school, of some of the results that had been accomplished, and of what can be done in the future.

4. Quartet—"Twilight Bells"—Jennie Hopper, Jennie Hill, Mabel Houts, and....................................Anna Lightfoot
5. Essay—"The Mission of Nations"..................Ella Gillespie

The mission of the Greek nation was to give to the world fine arts and literature. Rome's mission was the arts of war. The Roman law was elastic, and 'hence made room for progress. England's mission is the acquiring of wealth. The mission of the United States is freedom to the world.

6. Discussion—"Shall we Return the Phillipines?" Affirmative, Renzo Muckleroy. Negative.................T. B. F. Smith

The first speaker gave four things that could be done with the islands. 1. Give them back to Spain. 2. Give them their freedom. 3. Give them to other nations. 4. Keep them ourselves. After presenting the usual arguments on the first three, the speaker concluded that the fourth was stronger than either of the others. The speaker took up two points, principally. the argument against imperialism, or that the Constitution did not give us any warrant for acquiring new territory. The second was that the right of government came from the consent of the governed.

7. Piano Duet—"Valse Tyrolienne"....Bertha Spence, Ethel Crouse
8. Recitation—"The Light on Dead Man's Bar,"..... Nellie Thornton

The rendering of this was fine.

9. Oration—"Illinois.".........................Thomas J. Layman

Illinois is a wonderful state. Mr. Layman spoke of the early exploration of Illinois by LaSalle and Joliet, and the work of Marquette among the Indians. Now the state ranks second to none in educational affairs. Shurtleff College was founded more than seventy years ago. Less than seventy miles from Carbondale stands "Old Kaskaskia," or did before it was washed away by the water of the Mississippi, the site of the first capital of the state. In time of war, both in the late war with Spain and the war of the rebellion, Illinois has shown her patriotism by responding nobly to the call on her for men. Among the great men she has furnished the nation stand Lincoln, Grant and Logan.

10. Chorus — Misses Jennie Hopper, Jennie Hill, Mabel Houts, Anna Lightfoot; Messrs. Arthur Lee, Frank Mackey, E. B. Vaughn, and............ ....T. B. F. Smith

The song, "Jubilee," was acted as well as sung, and was excellent.

11. Oration—"Problems of the Age," and Presentation of Diplomas............ ..../......J. Oscar Marberry

Every age has its problems that are peculiar to it. Every nation has its own problems that are its own heritage. In this day of American progress this nation has its problems, two of which were specially mentioned; first, the problem of labor and capital. The history of the past few years is a story of the conflict between these two forces; a story of the conflict between the strong and the weak. Second: Increase of population in our large cities is followed by an increase of crime. Both of these problems must be met by a more complete system of education of the masses. At the close of the address the Seniors formed in a row and received at the hands of Mr. Marberry the diplomas from the Socratic Society given to those who were members.

12. Selections from...... ... ."Lady of the Lake."

A bower of leaves had been prepared on the stage large enough for all the performers of the evening. Now the curtain was run down in front of this bower, all but the electric light extinguished, and a magic lantern light so arranged that it could be thrown on the bower. Costumes had been procured for those who were to take part in the pantomime. Miss Lulu Whittenberg recited the "Lady of the Lake," or selections from the poem, and at points where it could be well illustrated by the characters in pantomime. The reading would stop, the lights turned off, the curtain rolled up, and the actors would be shown for about a minute in the exciting or interesting part of what had been recited. Then the curtain would be rung down, the lights turned on and the reciting resumed. It was well executed. The cast of characters was as follows:

Ellen Douglas...Anna Nelson
Earl Douglas...D. C. Jones
Roderick Dhu..Walter Stewart
James Fitz James.............,....................................S. Boomer
Malcolm Graeme..Roland Brinkerhoff

WEDNESDAY MORNING, JUNE 14.

The Alumni Association met in Socratic Hall to participate in and listen to a program that had been prepared of reminiscences of the different classes in the past history of the school. Dr. J. T. McAnally, of the class of '78, took the chair at the appointed hour and called the meeting to order. After music by the orchestra, the the President called upon Miss May Wright, of Cobden, who was to represent the class of '76. After a few introductory remarks Miss Wright spoke of the different members of this class of five, the first class to graduate from the school. Mr. Beverly Caldwell has been teaching since his graduation, and is now at the head of the State Normal School of Louisiana. Mr. John C. Hawthorn studied law after his graduation, but only lived a few months after. Mr. George C. Ross taught for a number of years, but is now in the Department of the Interior at Washington. Miss Wright read a short but interesting letter from Mr. Ross. Miss Wright did not speak of the other member of the class, John C. Brown, but she said afterward that she had lost all trace of his whereabouts. In conclusion Miss Wright spoke of reminiscences of Dr. Allyn, and of a lesson the class learned from a class in drawing.

The class of '77 was represented by Hon. W. H. Warder, of Marion. He said in standing here it seems but a short time since Commencement day in 1877. The class of '77 was not so large as some classes that have graduated since, but they have been enthusiastic in doing the work they have been called upon to do. Miss Arista Burton has made a faithful teacher, and is still in the work in Colorado Springs, Colo. Mr. England taught for a time, but is now in the noble calling of a farmer near here. Miss Belle Barnes married Dr. H. H. Green, of Bloomington, and is now working in the high and noble sphere of wife and mother. A letter was read from Mrs. Green with regrets that she could not be with us to-day.

No one responded to the call of the class of '78.

When the class of '79 was called there was no response, and Miss Buck was called out to speak for that class. She said she had thought all the time she was a member of the Alumni, but had not known before what class she belonged to. The class was one of three classes who had only one woman in its number. In this case the one, Miss Ida McCreery, after teaching for three years, had been called to the higher life in the world above, Mr. A. C. Burnett, after graduating, studied law, but was now so busy with his bank affairs in Lamar, Mo., that he could not be here. George H. Farmer, after teaching several years in the state, went south, and is now teaching in Vandale, Ark. Mr. L. M. Phillips is enjoying the felicity of having married his second wife, and could not come. He is a dentist in Nashville, and finds so many teeth that need attention, and the care of the little girl who has no teeth so great that he readily finds an excuse for not being here.

The class of '80 was passed with no response.

The class of '81 was represented by Mr. John W. Lorenz, of Evansville, Ind. Mr. Lorenz said:

Fellow Alumni, Ladies and Gentlemen:

It has always been a most undesirable task for me to make an address, but when this call came to say a few words for my class on this occasion, I rejoice to do it.

The class I represent is the one which graduated in '81. Just eighteen years ago all of us received our diplomas and departed for our various fields of labor.

We were an unusually good class. There is nothing surprising about it. We had studied Natural History according to the "*French*" method; we had gone to "*Rome*" for our Latin and Greek; we had been "*Foster*"-ed in Geography, History and Physiology, and had "*Hull*"-ed all the theorems and problems of Higher Mathematics. Besides this we relished and cherished a long list of other studies, among which were the wonderful phenomena of Physics and Chemistry under the man who started at the lowest round of the pedagogic ladder by teaching a lonely district school. By diligent attention to duty, performing each to the best of his ability, he rose, step by step, to the highest round, and is to-day the honored President of this justly famous Southern Illinois Normal University.

I have always admired this class. We could all live in the same little village and competition among the various vocations be the very keenest, yet there would be no animosity among us. Ours would only be that noble emulation to see which one can do the most good. *No two of us follow the same occupation.*

We have, among our number, the lawyer and statesman, the financier and banker, the devout minister, the farmer, who is one of the corner-stones of national prosperity; the surveyor, who tells us how far our real estate extends, and, last but not least, the *sine qui non*, the one without which everything is nothing—the uncrowned queen of the home.

We did wisely in first obtaining a collegiate education before starting on our life work. It has been to us what the giant-minded Cicero, about two thousand years ago, so tersely said: "Education fosters youth, delights old age, secures prosperity, furnishes a place of refuge and solace in adversity; it is a joy at home, no impediment when abroad, passes the night with us, and is a a companion in our walks and in our recreations."

We are enthusiastic believers in popular education, and hope the time not far distant when every child in this extraordinary land of ours will get, not only a common school education.

Next to that, each child should be made a study as to what it is best fitted for, and allowed to pursue that vocation for which it is best qualified by nature, or for which it has the most desire. You who are judges of horses can tell at once whether a certain animal would be most serviceable for a buggy or for heavy draught, and it is accordingly bought or sold for that purpose. Give the human subject the same careful consideration in that respect, and you will have an age in which every man and woman is happy and prosperous in the pursuit of his or her work, and attaining the greatest success possible.

Thus laboring, pursuing, achieving, rejoicing, onward our life journey goes, each one so living that when that summons comes to join the innumerable caravan that moves to those glorious realms, we go, not like the quarry slave at night, scourged to his dungeon, but sustained and soothed by an unfaltering trust, we approach our graves like those who "wrap the drapery of their couch about them and lie down to pleasant dreams."

When the class of '82 was called Mrs. W. H. Livingston, of Pana, responded with an excellent paper: "To those of us who were present at the laying of the corner-stone of this State Normal that bright May day in 1870; to us and to the teachers who began this work twenty-five years ago, this week shows an abundant harvest from so small a seed. These six days of jubilee will not suffice to give a summary or a synopsis of the great work done for the state of Illinois by this school since that spring day." Mrs. Livingston gave some reminiscences then of the laying of the corner-stone, in which she mentioned the little sprig of evergreen that was placed in the little box, and of the fulfillment of what it was intended to symbolize in the faithful work done here. The silent influence of the building in the betterment of school architecture, was also spoken of. Then followed mention of some of the members of the class. Adella Goodall, now Mrs. Dr. Mitchell, of Carbondale, is one who cordially welcomes back the old students, those of her class and others. Wezette Atkins, now Mrs. C. W. Parkinson, is at present at home in Carbondale, but in the fall will remove to Edwardsville, where her husband is to be Superintendent of Schools. Arthur E. Parkinson is in business in Chicago. Dr. H. A. Stewart is also a resident of Chicago, where he has a lucrative practice. Lizzie Deardorf, now Mrs. DeMoss, in Ballard, a suburb of Seattle, is busy looking after her household duties and a seven-year-old son. Mr. Albert Mead is a lawyer, of Blaine, Washington, but his home is in New Whatcom.

He is well spoken of in the New Whatcom Reveille, the paper published by Prof. Hull. Mr. W. J. Ennison is now a lawyer in Hartford, Conn. Mr. John W. Wood, so long a teacher, has at last, he says, accidentally changed work, and is now a merchant in Floresville, Texas. After some more reminiscences of schooldays and faculty, Mrs. Livingston closed with a poem that was one of Dr. Allyn's favorites—"Rain on the Roof."

There was no response when the classes of '83 and '84 were called.

For the class of '85 Mr. J. P. Gilbert, of McLeansboro, sang a solo.

Class of '86 was responded to by Mrs. J. J. Irvin, of Edwardsville. Mrs. Irvin was known here in school as Miss Louella Nichols. Mrs. Irvin entered the Normal in the fall of 1883, and on November 26 of that year occurred the fire that destroyed the first building. She was in the drawing-room working as one of a class on a picture. How well she remembered those ducks, and how hard she worked to get them on paper, her first picture. It was lost in the fire with the Normal building. Her class of thirteen was the last to graduate in the tent out on the campus. Mrs. Irvin spoke of several members of her class, closing with mention of Edgar L. Storment, who had so recently passed away to his work in the upper world. He would no more meet with us here on earth, but we could meet with him. A. H. Fulton is now County Superintendent of Schools at Phœnix, Arizona.

D. J. Cowan, of Vienna, Ill., responded to the call for the class of '87. The class of '87 was the largest but one of any class that has been graduated from the Normal, containing twenty-eight. The class of '97 numbered twenty-nine. As with the other classes, while nearly all had taught since graduating, the class now contained in its ranks lawyers, doctors, railroad agents, one editor, one County Judge, one—Miss May Cleveland—a trained nurse, and our genial friend, Cicero Hawkins, who should have spoken for the class to-day, is State's Attorney for Perry county. Our class is all right and is proud of its Alma Mater, the Southern Illinois Normal, and the work she is doing. In 1889 I was in New Whatcom, Washington, little thinking that I should find any one I knew in that part of the country, when who should come up with hand extended but James H. Kirkpatrick? Meeting him at that time where I was a stranger was a greater pleasure than meeting with all of you here to-day. Mr. Kirkpatrick is still teaching. I spent seven years on the Pacific coast.

There was no response to the call for the class of '88. W. H. Hall, of Chicago, had been expected to give reminiscences of his class, but was not here.

William Wallace, of Charleston, was down on the program for the class of '89, but not responding, Superintendent Walter King, of Tamaroa, was called out to speak for the class. His first reminiscence was of the times they used to have in the Socratic Society when he was a member. "It was a fact that if there was a fight on hand in society work I was in it. Just before graduating Dr. Allyn called the class into the reception room and pinned a small bouquet of daisies onto the coat or dress of each one, and said, 'This is the daisy class.' Of the class I can say but little. Miss Parks is here in the Training Department; Miss Lois Allyn, after teaching four years, married and is now Mrs. Mason, of Winchendon, Mass." He here read a letter from Mrs. Mason. Mrs. Mamie Bridges was married and is living in Missouri. Mr. J. D, McMeen was at Jonesboro, but he did not know where he was now.

MUSEUM.

**LIBRARY
OF THE
UNIVERSITY OF ILLINOIS**

There was no response when the class of '90 was called.

Miss Addie Hord, of Murphysboro, read the following poem when her name was called to represent the class of '91:

THE CLASS OF '91.

Backward, turn backward, O time, if you may,
Bring back our school life just for to-day;
Classmates, come back to this dear spot once more,
We'll laugh and be happy the same as of yore.

Wear on thy foreheads no shadow of care,
Smiles and glad voices must be everywhere;
No frowns, doubts, nor fears, for there surely were none
Found on thy faces in the days of 'ninety-one.

Backward, flow backward, O tide of the years,
We're tired of the school-room, its toils and its tears:
Toil richly recompensed, tears not in vain,
But take them and give us our school days again.

Then we were happy, light-hearted and free,
With never a thought, Alma Mater, but thee;
We loved thee so well that not one could brook
A frown from the Doctor, cross word or look.

Over our lives in the days that have flown,
But few so care free ever have shown;
We laughed at our lessons, yet often we sighed,
When on our papers a low grade we spied.

Our work in school or society hall,
Has left, I'm sure, sweet memories for all,
Which through sorrows or pleasures, long will cling,
Tenderly cherished in the hearts of eighteen.

Tho' happily passed our school terms away,
We longed the while for graduation day.
But when at last the longed for time had come,
Closing the work for the class of 'ninety-one,

It seemed to us then that we could not tear
Our lives from the ties which held us there;
And into our hearts a sadness came,
Knowing as a class we'd ne'er meet again,

"We plant for the ages," our motto so grand,
We tho't quite worthy so loyal a band;
"We plant for the ages," our motto was then;
It might be "We help," could we choose it again.

We felt in this life we'd a great work to do,
Must prove to the world we were loyal and true.
Has the world been startled? 'Twas by the sound
Of our ideals as they fell to the ground.

Perhaps many hopes lie crushed at our feet,
The lessons they taught, tho' bitter and sweet,
Did we seek to win with too great a zest,
And find that our talents would not stand the test?

The student builds castles for future day—
The teacher smiles as they vanish away;
But peace, sweet peace, into our lives may creep
If content to sow for others to reap.

Classmates, dear classmates, we'll gather to-night
And clasp our hands with an old-time delight;
A happy reunion, yet happier still,
If every member his place could fill.

With, classmates, loved President and teachers gone,
Whose faces we miss from among the throng,
There can not be, till our life work is done,
A perfect reunion of the class of 'ninety-one.

John W. Emerson, of Albion, was next called upon to speak for the class of '92. He said:

"Seven years ago the class of '92 launched forth from this haven. Our little barks have been scattered in every direction by wind, wave and current. Some have found a safe harbor in distant ports, others of us have anchored near the shore; but ever the trembling pennants of our hearts have looked back to this fair isle we left. And to-day, as we gather in fraternal reunion, our minds are busy with the memories of days that are past.

"I shall not endeavor this morning to indulge in reminiscences of those times that are gone. Pleasant and profitable were those days, and long shall we cherish them in our hearts. I desire to speak a few words in behalf of those teachers who gave their best energies that we might become leaders of thought in the communities in which we lived. Some have passed beyond the river. Some have removed to other fields; and yet a few still remain faithfully toiling that the youth of Southern Illinois may become wiser and better. Have these teachers left no monument by which the memories of their work shall be perpetuated? Over the inner entrance of St. Paul's cathedral, London, you may read the epitaph of C. Wren, its architect. It is this: 'Reader, if thou desirest his monument, look around you.' That, my friends, is the epitaph of the teacher of the Southern Illinois Normal. 'If thou desirest his monument, look around you.' Not at this beautiful building and its modern equipments, but at the trained young men and women who in nearly every community of our section are working out the problems of higher destiny. Honor, then, it will be, my fellow alumni, when our summons comes to join the 'innumerable caravan' to leave upon this prairie sod of Illinois a memorial similar to that which they have erected.

"Seven years ago the class of '92, consisting of twenty-two members, completed their course at this institution and received their diplomas from one who had spent a long and useful life in the cause of education. For more than half a century he had labored to better equip young men and women in the complex duties of life that they might become an honor to themselves and a blessing to humanity. It is but fitting that the class of '92 should give special honor to that President whose career as President ended just when we completed our course. Dr. Allyn lives to-day in the hearts of those who in his later years went out from the portals of this institution. Impossible is it for us to measure the good that this revered schoolmaster has done. Through his influence homes were made happier, schools better, and communities stronger. He lighted the land of Egypt with the purer light of intelligence and morality. Nor is his beneficent influence confined to the past. His earthly form has been laid away, but the influence of his noble character lives on, and will continue to live on and on, down the generations, blessing mankind and shedding its rays of hope and love all along the pathway of humanity.

"Truly has it been said that the greatest teachers of humanity are the lives of our great men. They are a never-failing source of inspiration, and, guided by their example, we may become wiser and better.

"And to-day let us. not forget another who was an ever-ready helper in our times of need. His cheery words and jovial spirit drove away the shades of despondency. His song and story lightened the cares of school life, and his friendly counsel and generous aid helped us over many of the rough places of our school career. Prof. S. M. Inglis has been called to his reward; but 'to live in hearts we leave behind is not to die.' He has left his impress on the schools of our state; he has left his impress on the hearts of his pupils and his countrymen.

"Members of the class of '92, let the good that these men have done be an inspiration to us. Let the example of those yet living prompt us to greater actions and nobler endeavor. Let us by word and encouragement show our appreciation of their efforts. Let us from year to year gather here in annual reunion to recount the pleasant experiences of the past, and renew our allegiance to our Alma Mater. Let us do more than this. Let us pledge the best energies of our lives for the furtherance of the cause for which this institution was founded —for the cause which is rapidly making 'Egypt' no longer a by-word and reproach, but is making it a synonym for intelligence, prosperity and happiness."

When the class of '93 was called, Miss Sarah Whittenberg, of Vienna, responded:

"What of the class of '93? Though our roll boasts the historic names of Brown and Curtis, a Davis and a Moore, we know of no story of remarkable achievement with which to entertain you. We recall nothing in the history of our class, when connected with our Alma Mater, to justify a hope that we would startle the world with a Marconi, a Kippling, or a Funston, or a Dewey. Yet in earnestness of purpose, in plodding perseverence, and in the quiet virtues that make up the character of the typical American citizen, we're not found wanting.

"When organized, having in our minds the rather stormy career of a sister class, we inscribed upon our banner the watchword 'Peace,' and save some slight skirmishing occasioned by the conflicts of our wills with that of the powers that were, we were true to our resolution. Thus favored with domestic tranquility, and with most pleasant relations toward our honored faculty and fellow students, the remembrance of our sojourn in the university is fraught with many very precious recollections. Among the most precious of these are those in which the venerable and much loved Dr. Allyn figured. Except during our senior year it was our privilege to be connected with the university during his presidency. I would be but giving expression to an experience common to very many whom I address should I relate instances in which he manifested scarcely less than a father's interest in our welfare. My classmates will enjoy living over with me again the following incident: For some time there had been an uncertainty as to who shall select the minister to preach the baccalaureate sermon. Finally the question is decided and the choice is left to us. With one mind we selected Dr. Allyn; and at an appointed time repair in a body to his home to make known formally our wishes. He kindly welcomed us, accepted our invitation, surprised us with refreshments provided for our pleasure, and for an hour graciously entertained us. A few Sabbaths later we listened to the last baccalaurate address delivered by Dr. Allyn. Before another year passed he had joined the company of the immortal.

"We would not fail in these reminiscences, gratefully to recall the other members of the faculty from 1888 to 1893. Of these Professors Hull, Buchanan, Hall, Rocheleau and Misses Finley, Robarts, Green, Anderson and Mrs. Way have entered other fields of labor. Professor Inglis has joined Dr. Allyn in the home above. To the memory of each one of these, and those who are now connected with the university, the class of '93 is loyal.

"Returning to the halls of our Alma Mater on this, her twenty-fifth anniversary, we are not an unbroken band. Even the first year of our separation death claimed for his own one whose manly, Christian character had been an inspiration to us. A life full of promise seemed to have been ended all too soon, yet the brief career of Charles L. Stout brought a blessing to the world.

"Numbering sixteen, representing fourteen counties in Illinois and one in a distant state, and serving in six honorable avocations, we, the class of '93, hope to bear honorably our share of the responsibility which rests peculiarly on the Alumni of the Southern Illinois Normal University—the responsibility of wielding an influence that will so mould public sentiment as to make Southern Illinois the peer of any section of our great state, or, indeed, of the nation."

Class of '94 was represented by a solo by Miss Harriet Jenkins, of Evansville, Ind.

Class of '95, not represented.

Class of '96— George D. Wham, of Olney, responded to the call of his name:

"First of all, I esteem it a privilege to speak for the class of '76. It is a double honor, both from the occasion, the first of its kind in the history of the school, and from the character of the class, which embodies as much real manhood and womanhood as could be found in any class, not only of this, but any other institution. The class of '96 was a good example of unity in diversity.

We were of all ages, sizes, complexions, temper and temperament; and yet no class, perhaps, discharged its class duties with better agreement and good feeling.

"I will not try to rehearse the various experiences of my class, although they were new to us then and dear to us now. I do not suppose we escaped the vanities or blundering of other classes, and our ups and downs were your ups and downs, with modifications of circumstances.

"Like the alumni of other years, we have kept our eyes turned toward the Normal, eagerly watching for every sign of progress. Our strongest and best reason for this is the affection we feel for an institution that has been to us a kind, fostering mother. Generally speaking, we graduates are judged by what the school is now, and not by its standard when we graduated. If the school improved, our prestige as graduates increases accordingly. If the school goes down, we will get less credit from the public than we deserve. Thus for two reasons—love for our Alma Mater, and love for ourselves—we are inspired with an anxiety to see the Normal making steady and rapid progress. And in these brief three years we have not been disappointed.

"A criterion of success in a Normal is to be found in the attitude of its graduates toward the profession of teaching, and the ultimate question is whether or not it sends forth professional teachers who desire to teach for the sake of teaching, and who feel there is something more to be desired than salary. I think there are two indications that such a work is being done in the Southern Normal. One is that of recent years more students than before expect to make teaching their profession. While this condition exists there will be less speculation at lunch hour about medicine and law, and more earnest effort in the class room to getting ready for the business of teaching. A second reason is that graduates are not so anxious to become superintendents of schools. The time was when a subordinate position was looked upon with scorn, and the Senior set his stakes at once for some position of prominence and salary. Not that any of us would particularly avoid such a position now, but the sentiment is changing, and has already changed. An evidence of this condition is the demand for High School positions. I am told that a majority of the graduates of the last few years choose to become teachers of special subjects where actual teaching can be done. It certainly is an indication of great significance that the students here are so developing that they are willing, regardless of immediate reward, to serve wherever they can do the most effective work."

There was no response when the class of '97 was called.

For the class of '98 Miss Margery Wilson, of Carlyle, responded:

"One of the speakers spoke of his class being the 'daisy' class. The class of '98 also had the daisy as its floral emblem. What is the real value we get from a Normal school? In the great universities where the number of students is large, the personal contact of student and teacher is lost. Our school is not large, but there is a personal influence goes out from teacher to pupil, and I like it."

Miss Wilson spoke of the influence the true teacher might have upon the "giggling girl and the fighting boy."

"There is a certain stage in the adolescence of youth when a girl will giggle, not specially because she has something to laugh at, but because at this period of adolescence it is her nature to do so. It is useless to try to suppress the giggle, but try to so direct the child that there is an appreciation of her surroundings, and show her that there is really much that may provoke mirth, and much that is more serious. In the pugnacious age of the boy, try to lead him to fight, instead of his playmates, his evil passions and impulses."

WEDNESDAY EVENING.

At about six o'clock the Alumni, Faculty, Board of

Trustees and friends assembled in the gymnasium, where tables had been set for two hundred guests, and the annual Alumni banquet was held. After a reasonable time had been devoted to a feast of the good things that had been prepared, and those present had enjoyed a period of social intercourse, the President of the association, Dr. J. T. McAnally, acting as toastmaster, called for responses to sentiments given from several present. Mr. C. W. Bliss was asked to speak in behalf of the former Board of Trustees: First, he was not in extra condition for a speech; had reached Carbondale about two o'clock the morning before; no bed to be found at the hotel, but was given a lounge; in the morning he found he had been sleeping on a relief map of Colorado, head perched on Pike's Peak, feet on Marshall's Pass, while his body lay in the Royal Gorge. Did not come one hundred and fifty miles to make a speech, but to see the members of the old Board, who were to be here. Several stories were told to illustrate as he went along. One of the things the old Board did was to build the science building within the appropriation given by the state, which was not done by any other Board in the state. Our system of education, both High school and lower grades, is open to the criticism that it gives the child a great many subjects, but does not give him enough of any of them.

Mrs. Mary Ogden was called upon to respond for the Faculty of the past. Mrs. Ogden began in the Model school, passed on up from there to the Normal, and graduated; taught eight years, then married, and has now a home and two children to care for. She had visions of Prof. Hillman, the teacher of Arithmetic; visions of gathering in front of his home and hearing "Hark, Orcelia, we're being serenaded." Visions of Prof. Foster, the teacher of Physiology; of his being called from the class one day to find, on his return, that the class were not in quite the order they were when he left them a moment before. "What! Such behavior in this class!" Visions of Miss Mason, the teacher of the Training Department; Miss Buck, serene in her back room, surrounded by her boys and girls—we thought she gave more attention to the boys than to us. Visions of Mrs. Nash, the teacher of Drawing: "Now, George, what are you doing?" Visions of Dr. Thomas trying to teach a class of mischievous children: "Now, children, I shall have to take a stick to you if you don't behave." "I was asked to become a member of the Faculty during the time school was held in the temporary building. Dr. Allyn came to me and said that some of the teachers had more than they could do, and needed help; would I come down the next morning and help them? I came. My work during the years I taught gave me great insight into the keen perception of that grand man. He never asked a thing of his teacher that he thought could not be done. He praised, but not in flattery. He might give work that seemed beyond our ability to do, but which we did do."

Prof. Kirk was called upon to speak for the present Faculty:

"I esteem very highly the tribute to address such a representative body as this. We are like trees. 'By their fruits shall ye know them.' This term five hundred and thirty persons have been enrolled in the school, and we graduate a class of twenty-two. We are not to be looked upon, as to the good we do, by the size of the class we graduate, for more than twenty times the size of the class have come under the school's influence. We might compare our pupils, as they go out, to inanimate objects of nature, some of them subject to the influences of their surroundings more than others. Those who are intellectually strongest are least subject to their surroundings. Men without character are most subject to such influences, and accomplish least in life; men of character accomplish the most. I have compared this school with other institutions, and the comparison is not to the discredit of this school. This school's individuality has wrought righteousness in the heart. So long as I see here men who rely on God's direction, the school is going to prosper. Holland said 'a time like this demands men.' All times demand men of strong minds, ready hands and steady hearts."

State Superintendent Alfred Baylis was next called upon to speak for the present Board of Trustees:

"If I were to say the first thing that comes into my mind I should say that, though nearly a stranger, I was associated as one of the members of the Faculty. Through her I learned much of the members of the Faculty, and learned to reverence Dr. Allyn." (To illustrate the greatness of this country, Supt. Baylis told a story of a Britisher who became acquainted with an American on a voyage from London to New York. On reaching New York the Londoner said to his companion that he had a friend, Henry, in San Francisco, and another friend, John, in Chicago, and that after breakfast he believed he would go to see Henry and stop over a few minutes to see John, but would be back to lunch with him. On reaching the station he asked for a round-trip ticket to San Francisco, with a stop-over at Chicago. While the agent was folding up the long roll of ticket he asked the price, and was thunder-struck when told. 'Well, how far is it?' The agent gave him the figures—over 3,000 miles—when he fainted. Recovered in a short time enough to say, 'Merciful heavens, what a great country!' and then go off in another faint.) "It is a great country. Perhaps the development is greater since the founding of this institution. In my early life boys used to leave college, go to Southern Illinois and Missouri in the beginning of the wheat harvest to help cradle and bind the grain, working their way north to Michigan, and making money enough to take them through the next year in school. Now there is a great change. The twine binder has taken the place of the cradle." (Another instance of progress was spoken of.) "Some boys took sardine cans and found that by carefully taking out one side and fastening a string to the other, with a can on each end of a string, and the string stretched, they could talk over the string so as to be understood. But little did these boys think that in a short time the modern telephone would take the place of the sardine cans and string. A few months ago war was declared with Spain. The soldiers who volunteered were young, and it was said that these young fellows would not make soldiers. But they did make soldiers, and brought the war to a speedy close. Young manhood has maintained the prestige of the past. This is the work of schools. The business of the teacher is to develop manhood. The duty of this school is to prepare teachers to do this work. Use the money given by the state to the best advantage, in a way that will make the most of it. The school is now twenty-five years old. One of the strongest allies to the Carbondale school are the undergraduates. If the Alumni and these stand by it, it will be maintained."

Here the banquet adjourned to Normal Hall, where addresses were given by Prof. G. V. Buchanan, of Sedalia, Mo., and ex-Lieutenant Governor Joseph B. Gill, of San Brenardino, Cal.

It was hoped that the entire addresses could be printed in this volumn, but the committee was driven to the painful duty of making but a brief reference to the subject matter as presented by the honored members of the Alumni Association.

ALUMNI ADDRESSES.

Prof. George V. Buchanan, class of '84, took for his topic "Dick Olmstead, an Average American Boy, Reared Under Average American Conditions:"

The hero of the address was born amid the simplest environments of a frontier home in the Mississippi Valley. His parentage was of such a type as to secure for the young lad such a character as was needed to meet the untoward surroundings of his early life and prepare him for the highest usefulness in later years. Being born into a family of older children, this little group was a miniature state in its varied interests and the solution of many problems of equity and justice.

The speaker followed the little urchin through the years of childhood, boyhood, young manhood and maturity, showing the salient influences that are so patent in the proper development of the individual, claiming that there are two giant forces playing upon the life for weal or woe—heredity and environment. With the first the teacher has little to do; with the second much more.

The mother has much to do with the spiritual development of the child, and so has the primary teacher. Froebel and Pestalozzi were reformers in this respect. Within the last decade a new impetus has been given to the study of the individual child. Due honor was paid to the work of the kintergarten in the early teaching of children.

The address was replete with wholesome truths that proved the speaker to be a thoughtful student of the problem of the proper training of the child through the various stages of his development. He paid a fitting tribute to the loyal and hopeful mother who retained her faith in her thoughtless boy when all other friends had deserted him. The story of the youth preparing to leave home for the academy, his life there, his graduation, and later his experience in college, the study of law, his success in the practice of his profession, his marriage, the beautiful family he gathered around him, the first shadow that flitted across his pathway in the long illness and finally the death of a devoted daughter, followed by a decided growth of Christian character and enlargement of soul power, was portrayed in a most charming manner. The hearers were led to see that the most critical time in life of this noble character was when the destiny was largely in the hands of the devoted mother and faithful teachers. The speaker closed with the following forceful utterances: "Many noble boys are smothering worthy ambitions for need of far-sighted friendships to point them to the star of possibility. Let us highly resolve to direct American youth to the royal road of honor; to that big highway, which is paved with honesty, industry and perseverance, where living is not drifting but is manly strife in spirited contest; where great characters are developed in the heat of action, and where the thrill of honest effort is a constant stimulus to greater exertion."

Hon. Joseph B. Gill, class of '84, ex-Lieutenant Governor of Illinois, spoke on the "History of Alumni" (Limited).

The highly appreciated address began by an allusion to the visit of Saturn to Italy, where a citadel was founded. In recent times, by statutory enactment, representatives of the empire state of Illinois came to Carbondale and founded the Southern Illinois Normal University.

Having passed through a history of twenty-five years, it is fitting, said the speaker, that some recognition be given to those who have completed the courses of study during this time and added the luster of their lives to the glory of the last quarter of a century of the world's history. The number of our association now entitles it to consideration and honored recognition. Those who have been the most successful have had the hardest battle.

A hasty review was given to the effect of the influence of so large a company of cultured men and women being distributed throughout the length and breadth of the land.

The honored speaker referred to the many improvements made in the buildings, grounds, and general equipment of the institution. He dwelt upon the modern style of writing names; instead of the John S. Brown graduate of former years he becomes John Sherman Brown; the J. C. B. Jones changes to John C. Babbington Jones; the Mary J. Smith, after marriage, transforms to the hyphenated Marie Janet Smythe-Trope." The first movements of the graduate is marked by the utmost grace and charming precision. With head erect, step elastic, easy manners, courtly grace, and bewitching smile, he is in love with himself and at peace with the whole world."

The speaker in his inimitable style, pictured the graduate in his first attempt at making a living.

"From the unstilled seas on the north to the American dependences in the south, and from the Atlantic across the continental divide to the Pacific you will find the normal graduate, whose expansion is second only to that of his country."

Mr. Gill showed that the Alumni had entered all of the professions and had, with few exceptions, reflected credit upon their Alma Mater. The great bulk have been and are teachers, "which is the highest compliment." They have been gradually promoted till many of them occupy positions of merit and honor. The ministers have diligently sown tne seed and harvested golden results. The editors are not a few, "moulders of public opinion." The lawyers are not wanting; "they put asunder what the ministers put together." They are exceedingly reserved and advance rapidly; the client does the "advancing," and the lawyer handles the "reserve." Physicians are numerous; their fees are reasonable considering the valuable services rendered. Patients "are in the hands of their friends" when they appeal to our doctors. The merchant, the farmer, and the politician are not wanting, each filling a needed place in the community in which they strive. "Love of country and true patriotism are emblazoned on our banner. Our volunteer soldiers climbed San Juan Hill for the sake of humanity, and crossed the rivers in the Philippines in horseless carriages, or otherwise, to prevent the cannibals of these islands from eating each other." In closing the speaker said: "Everything augers well; let it be said in the future, as now and heretofore, that we have not proved recreant to our trust, but at all times and under all conditions have lived honorable lives and been worthy of our beloved institution."

THURSDAY MORNING, JUNE 15.

At ten o'clock the Faculty, Seniors, Board of Trustees and distinguished visitors marched from the President's office to the platform in Normal Hall under the direction of Prof. S. E. Harwood. After the music, and invocation by Rev. J. W. Parkhill, of the Presbyterian church, Dr. Parkinson introduced Emerson E. White, LL. D., of Columbus, O., as the orator of the day. Reference was made to the authorship of White's series of Mathematics, but more recently a writer of pedagogical works, and his leadership in educational matters in the nation.

Dr. White spoke on "The Duty of the Hour:" "Childhood is a warfare. On the one side are reason and conscience; on the other are a gang of animal appetites, which, says Mann, are of the nature of beasts and birds of prey. But not more fierce are the battles that may be seen in an eagle's nest than in the warfare be-

**LIBRARY
OF THE
UNIVERSITY OF ILLINOIS**

tween the passions in the breast of a child. What so sweet as a darling little babe; and yet the sweet babe became the bloodthirsty Nero. If in the development of the child the higher nature is made to conquer, then the life is one of honor and usefulness; if on the other hand the lower nature conquers, then the life is one of shame. In this we see that, though there are great possibilities in the life of a child, the mere possession of such possibilities clothed in a god-like nature is not the fruition.

It is not necessary that the child be born to affluence; the highest achievements of the human race have been by those born in obscurity and poverty. Charles the Fourth of France was the son of a peasant girl. In our own country it was the poor boy who struck the shackles from four millions of slaves, and took his high place in history.

There are three voices to be heard in the cry of every child. Whose duty is it to hear these voices and respond to them? It is the duty of the parents to respond to the first of these voices. They are God's vice-regents on earth, charged with a duty to train the child, and they can not shirk this responsibility. A few years ago I heard a brilliant lecture on "Home, Sweet Home," which was infamous. The speaker asserted that marriage is a contract, and hence the parties making the contract had a right to annul it. Marriage may be in one sense a contract, but it is the only contract in the universe that brings a child into the world; and that takes it out of the list of ordinary contracts. The state is interested in the outcome of the bringing up of the child.

Second, the community in which a child is born is interested in the control and bringing up of the child. If the community could control the life of every child, crime would be lessened if not abolished. The state, as an enlarged and organized community, has an interest in the outcome of that child's bringing up, as the welfare of the state depends upon its being done properly.

Third, the property of the state should respond to the voice of the child. All the property in the state is under mortgage to educate that child, and a first mortgage, too. It is the only mortgage I know that increases the value of the property. Thus we see three agencies in the bringing up of every child—first, the family, second, the community, and third, the state with all its property. All these are in triple alliance for the preparation of that child for manhood. Besides these there is another potent agency, the church, that may and should have an influence on the life of the child. These are a summary of the arguments for universal education by the state.

Of the arguments that are brought forward one party asserts that the state has no right to educate—that belongs to the family. Another says that the state may educate in "three r's," but has no right to go any farther. But there are only two positions that can be defended in this argument. First, the state has no right to teach any branch. Second, the state has a right to teach any branch that may help humanity. There is no middle ground tenable. The state has either plenary right, or it has no right in the education of its realm.

The aristocracy sometimes assert that education is spoiling the youth. Carnegie affirms that we are over-educating our children. But the people do not consult the aristocracy in this matter, but know what they want.

In the last fifty years the nations of the world have been to school. My little arguments are weak enough when compared with what the nations have worked out.

First, the state must educate its citizens that it may be strong in war. In 1806 Napoleon I proclaimed war against Prussia, and after a decisive battle was able to dictate a treaty of peace. Frederick the Great shut himself in his castle sixty days and called a council. The verdict of the council was that Napoleon I had gained because of the superior intelligence of his army. The result was that as soon as the assembly could be called together an edict of universal education was passed. Prussia passed out of thought as a military power, but her schools were famous. In 1866 another war was declared. King William called together an army of 300,000 men, hurled them over the mountains of Bohemia, and the Austrian army was broken in pieces as the Prussian army had been crushed before. It was not the needle gun, but thought, that defeated Austria. What did Austria do? She put into her laws, as soon as a bill could be framed, compulsory education, that her children should be put into the schools. We will guarantee what the result will be.

Six more years passed when Napoleon III declared war against Prussia and was met by an army of 500,000 men called from the schools of Prussia. This army crossed into France and defeated the French. Who conquered at Sedan! Not the Prussian needle gun. Gambetta was not defeated by superior numbers, nor by superior generalship, nor by superior arms. In all these the French soldiers were the peer of their foes. On the Prussian side every man had at least a common school education; on the other side forty-five per cent. could not sign the pay roll. What did France do after her defeat? As soon as a law could be framed, passed one of the most complete systems of public education known in history. France appealed to the teacher to regain what she had lost in war. Now if France can keep her temper, and recent events seem to indicate she can, she is going to become a great nation.

Again, the little island country, Japan, accepted war with that hoary nation, China, whose population was numbered by hundreds of millions, and swept the Chinese from the seas in sixty days. Who conquered China? Twenty-five years ago Japan's school system was organized by two Americans. Every man in her army was educated to some extent at least, every officer was a scholar.

It is said by some one that the American marine has not an equal in the world. Meehan says naval battles are not won by ships; they are won by men. The American marine are not only intelligent, but they have a conscience.

Second, we must also educate that we may be prosperous in times of peace. The Indian builds his rude wigwam of one room, fashions his bow and arrows and is contented. Educate him and the rude wigwam gives place to the cottage and the bow and arrows are replaced by the implements of civilization. Everywhere, the world over, the ignorant live in hovels. Wherever you find a schooled people you find prosperity. Education promotes industry. Schooling makes labor more helpful and more productive. Horace Mann once asked several employers of large numbers of men in manufacturing establishments who in their employ, the educated or the uneducated, were the most skillful in their work, other things being equal. The replies were unanimous from the different employers that those who had at least a fair education were the most skillful. Schooled workmen rise in their grade of work, the ignorant sink. The schooled soon find themselves promoted to the higher class of work and better pay, work that is more difficult to perform yet lighter. Everywhere the business man recognizes that other things being equal the schooled man is the most proficient.

The year that the World's Fair was held in London Queen Victoria sent invitations to all the nations of the world, and the richest products of human workmanship were gathered from all nations in the great exhibition. These exhibits were classified in ninety departments. When the report on the awards was made known it was found that England had carried off the palm of excellence in all but ten departments of the ninety in the exhibition, and there was rejoicing all over England at the result.

Sixteen years passed over Europe, when Napoleon III sent forth his invitation to the nations, and the best products of human labor were gathered in Paris. These were divided into ninety departments as they had been in the great London exhibition. When the awards were given this time it was found that England had been victorious in but ten out of ninety departments, and that the United States had carried off prizes in twenty-seven departments, Prussia and France having the rest. A meeting was called in London to inquire into the cause of so few of the prizes going to that country. Why the great defeat? As a result of that meeting the Queen appointed a commission to inquire into the cause. The testimony of their commission was that England had been defeated at Paris by the schoolmaster. The evidence was that in the workshops and factories of victorious nations you do not find a machine tending a machine, but thought is tending the machine. The result of this was that as soon as a bill could be passed by Parliament there was established for the first time the school that compelled the children of the poor to be educated.

At the World's Fair at Vienna, twenty years later,

England rose in the scale of excellence of her exhibits. At the next meeting at Paris she rose still higher. At the Chicago World's Fair in 1893, the verdict is not known, but it is known that England stood well. Only one verdict has been seen, and from that we find that France led the world in the manufacture of artistic goods. When we consider that their common school system provides for courses of drawing, from the artistic standpoint this verdict is not to be wondered at, as this is taught to every child in the nation. Here I might say that during our late war with Spain it was thought for a time that France would join on the side of Spain. In some of the large cities of this country the leading women met and decided that in case France did side with Spain they would buy no more goods of French manufacture. The manufacturers of that country, seeing the danger to their trade, used their influence and the alliance was not formed. All nations are now appealing to the teacher that their workmen may be more skillful and that their manufactured products may find a market.

In my youth grain was cut with a sickle, the same kind of a tool that was used in the time of Boaz and Ruth, the grain being grasped in one hand and cut with the other, and it was possible for one man to cut about an eighth of an acre a day. Some ingenious Yankee conceived the idea that wooden fingers might take the place of the hand to grasp the grain, and the result was the invention of the square-cornered cradle. With this one man could cut an acre a day. But this was too heavy, and the next thought was to round off the corners and made the cradle lighter. With this one man could cut an acre and a half of grain in a day. Now, with the combined reaper and binder three men and a boy can cut and put up fourteen acres of wheat in a day, the boy to drive the team of three horses, and the three men to follow after and put the bundles into shocks.

To-day electricity and steam are used to draw our street cars in our large cities, and the horse and mule are put to other service. Before twenty-five years expire the powers of earth and air will be used to plow our fields and harvest our grain. Mind is going to relieve muscle, and do it skillfully. These are but illustrations of the effect of the schools on human industry.

The state must educate that human liberty may endure in the republic. The will of a people is law in a republic. It is all idle talk to maintain, as Matthew Arnold does, that a saving remnant or minority of intelligent people in a republic is sufficient. There must be a saving majority. A virtuous few can not leaven the lump of the American people. It must be a virtuous majority, and a large majority at that. Daniel Webster maintained that there were three conditions essential to the maintainance of the republic—first, universal education, second, a universal voting franchise, and third, proper distribution of landed property.

The ballot box must shape the destiny of our nation. When liberty is lost she will be buried in the tomb of intelligence. In the last presidential election the ballot was cast by more than one million who could not read or write. The salvation of the American republic is in the dispersion of the vast army of ignorance. Every child born under our flag must be prepared to meet the responsibilities of citizenship if our nation is to be perpetuated. We must see to it that there is a school for every child, and that every child is in the school. Nowhere do I say this with so much enthusiasm as in the south, where this question comes home to the people as to nowhere else.

Where the American flag goes in power, there the teacher must go with her primer. She must be a Christian teacher, too, if the masses are to be educated to meet the corruption of the times. What constitutes a state? Not cities and commonwealths, but MEN.

At the close of Doctor White's lecture Doctor Parkinson stated that for several years past it had been the custom for the President of the Board of Trustees to present the diplomas to the members of the graduating class. As the President of the Board, Judge Wheeler, could not be present at this time, he had asked State Superintendent Alfred Bayliss to take his place. Mr. Bayliss was then introduced to the audience and addressed the class:

"I regret the absence of the President of the Board, but as he is absent I am glad to have the honor of conferring diplomas on the class. I congratulate you on having completed your work in the school. The lecture we have just listened to is one of the strongest arguments possible for universal education. The idea is not new, but was as old as the counsels of the gods on the heights of Olympus. In response to who should be crowned as the greatest benefactor of mankind, first came the lawyer with his claim that he had prevented extortion and injustice; then came the doctor with his claim that he healed the wounds of mankind. So the minister and the laborer came, each with his claim of having benefited humanity. At last an aged man came, but presented no claim. When asked for his claim to be the greatest benefactor of mankind, he said he had no claim, but came with these, his pupils, to see to whom the award was given. At once Jupiter said, 'Crown him, crown the teacher as the greatest benefactor of the human race.'

"If the child has a mortgage on all the property of the state, as Doctor White argued, you are to collect the interest on the mortgage and see that it is properly expended in his education."

After the delivery of the diplomas Dr. Parkinson read letters from Hon. C. W. Terry, of Edwardsville, and Judge Wilkins, of Danville, expressing regrets that they could not be present on this jubilee occasion.

Faculty—Past and Present.

GRANVILLE F. FOSTER was a native of New Brunswick, where he received his early education, and taught four years. He came to Illinois in 1865 and taught in Sterling, Brighton and Du Quoin till he was elected to the chair of history and geography in 1874. He held this position nine years and then resigned to go west. He has since been constantly teaching in California. His home is in Berkeley, where his children have had the advantages of university training.

CYRUS THOMAS was born and educated in Tennessee. He came to Illinois in 1849 and began the practice of law in 1851. He was soon lured from this by his love of scientific pursuits, and connected himself with the U. S. Geological Survey of the Territories. Here he came in contact with the remains of pre-historic civilization, and then his life work was determined. He held the chair of natural science for six years, and at the same time was State Entomologist. In 1877 he was on the U. S. Commission to Investigate Locusts. In 1882 he was chosen to the department of ethnology in the Smithsonian at Washington, D. C. This position he filled many years. He has written several books which are accepted as authority by students of this subject.

ALDEN C. HILLMAN was one of the first Faculty, coming as principal of Preparatory Department and teacher of Arithmetic. He was a native of New York, where he received his education and began teaching. He came to

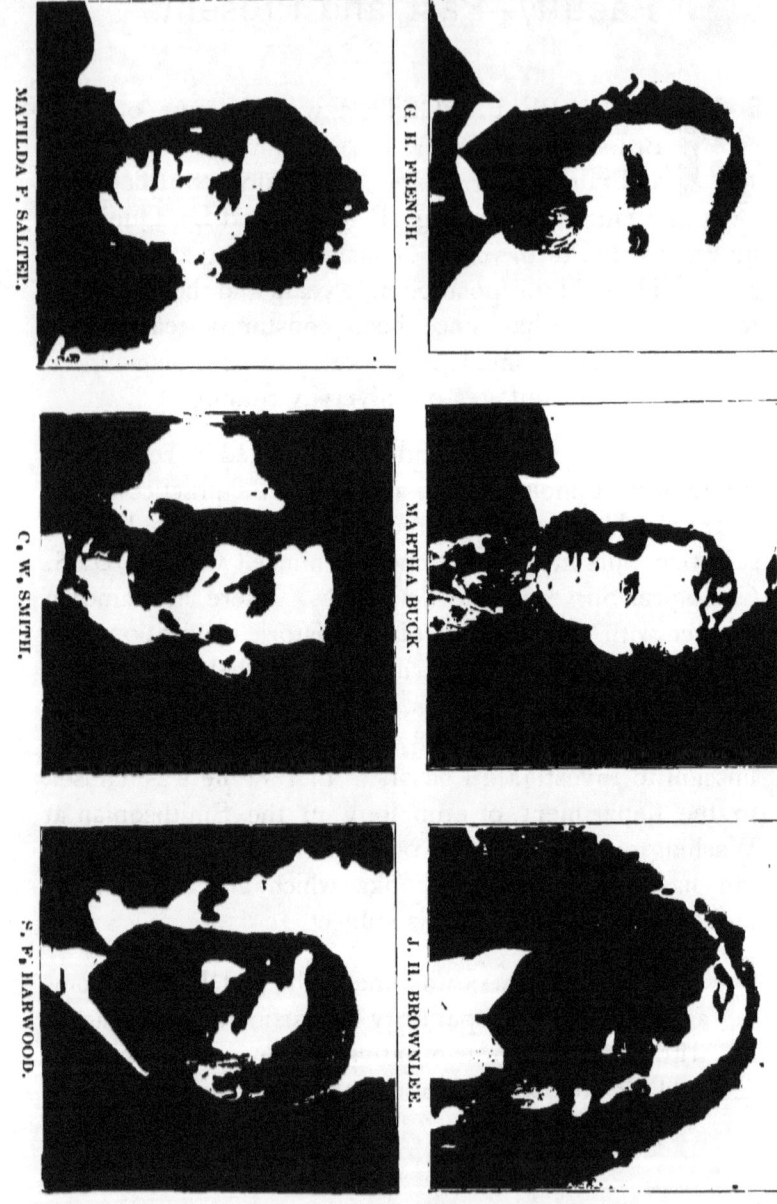

**LIBRARY
OF THE
UNIVERSITY OF ILLINOIS**

Illinois in 1855, and taught in our public schools till 1866, when he became Superintendent of Schools in Washington county. In 1871 he was chosen President of Illinois Agricultural College at Irvington, which place he resigned on the opening of the Southern Normal. He remained nine years, and resigned to seek a home in Salina, Kansas. Part of the time he has taught in that state, and he has been County Superintendent of Schools.

Jennie Candee was born in Indiana, but was educated at Galesburg, Illinois. She taught some years in the public schools, and in 1879 entered upon her duties as teacher of Drawing in the Southern Normal. In 1882 she resigned and married Mr. S. T. Brush, of Carbondale.

Mary A. Sowers, of the class of '81, had charge of the Training Department during the trying time of the fire. She is now Mrs. J. C. Scott, of Carbondale. Alice Krysher succeeded her in the Normal. She was of the class of '82, and is now Mrs. W. H. Livingston, of Pana, Illinois. As these ladies were graduates, further mention is found among the Alumni records. The same is true of Mary Wright, class of '76. She was valedictorian of her class, and when called to be assistant in Reading and Arithmetic in the opening of 1886 it was a disappointment that lack of health permitted her to remain but one term. She is now caring for her aged parents on the home farm near Cobden, Illinois.

Inez I. Green accepted the chair of geography in 1883, left vacant by the resignation of Mr. Foster. She held this position fourteen years. Before coming she had taught in Mount Vernon, Ill. She is now principal of the high school at that place.

On the resignation of Miss Raymond in 1884, LILLIAN B. FORDE was elected teacher of writing and drawing. She had received thorough training for her work in the schools of Boston, where she had resided. She remained but one year, but is still remembered for her excellent work and winning manners.

When Mr. Brownlee resigned in 1886 G. V. BUCHANAN, of the class of '84, was given the chair of mathematics. He had been a successful teacher before taking the course in the normal, and had done fine work as superintendent at Salem since his graduation. He remained seven years. Since that time he has been superintendent of schools in Sedalia, Mo.

MARY A. ROBARTS, class of '85, was employed as assistant in arithmetic and reading in 1886, and remained seven years. She is now Mrs. M. H. Ogden, of Carbondale.

LIZZIE M. SHEPPARD, class of '80, was given charge of the grammar school when it was separated from the primary grades in 1888, and held the position until she resigned in 1892, and married Dr. J. K. Miller, of Greely, Colorado.

MARY MCANALLY, class of '78, was engaged as assistant in 1888, and remained one year, when she resigned and married Mr. Norman A. Moss, of Mt. Vernon, Illinois.

W. H. HALL, class of '88, superintended the Carbondale public schools a year, and then took the chair of Arithmetic in the Normal. He held the position four years. He is now the business manager of Lewis Institute in Chicago. As the five last mentioned are all graduates, their records are found among the alumni of the school.

W. F. ROCHELEAU, a teacher of large experience and ability, came to the chair of Pedagogy and principal of the Training School when the place was left vacant by the promotion of Mr. Hull to the presidency of the Normal. He retained the position three years, resigning to seek a climate better suited to his health. He is the author of several excellent works, among them a fine series of readers. He has since been Superintendent of the Streator schools.

CHARLES W. JEROME, A. M.—Born September 8, 1838, in Onondaga county, N. Y. His father was a farmer, merchant and minister. Graduated from McKendree College in 1852. One of the founders of the Platonian Literary Society of that institution. After gradution he taught first in Danville and Shelbyville seminaries. Entered the Union army in 1862; was regimental quartermaster and first lieutenant. Mustered out in 1865. Returned to Shelbyville to resume charge of the seminary, where he remained till 1869, when he was elected principal of the Bedford Male and Female Seminary in Shelbyville, Tenn. Elected to the chair of Ancient Languages and registrar of the Southern Illinois Normal in 1874. This place he ably filled till the summer of 1890.

JULIA F. MASON—Born in Polo, Ogle county, Ill., July 13, 1853. Family moved to Normal in 1865 to educate the children. Graduated from the Illinois State Normal in June, 1872. Taught in the schools of Winchester and Lincoln the two years following. Elected to the principalship of the Model School in the Southern

Illinois Normal in September, 1874. Resigned December 8, 1876. Married D. B. Parkinson December 28, the same year. Died in San Jose, Cal., August 6, 1879. Buried in the cemetery of Bloomington, Ill. Her life was one of rare excellence and Christian beauty; her death peculiarly fitting one whose faith and trust had been unusually comforting.

MRS. HELEN M. NASH—Born in Vermont; educated in the public schools of her native state and in a Catholic convent at Washington, D. C. Maiden name was Rice. Husband a civil engineer. Elected to the chair of writing and drawing in the Southern Illinois Normal in September, 1876, which position she filled for three years. She possessed an ambitious spirit and a frail body, but was able by dint of great courage and persistence to accomplish much. She often said that she wished she were a man. Her friends have enjoyed a number of visits from her since her withdrawal from the school.

ESTHER C. FINLEY—Born in Lebanon, Ill., November 3, 1844. Father a teacher and minister; at one time the president of McKendree College. Graduated from the Presbyterian Academy, Jacksonville, Ill., in 1861. Taught in a private school in Lebanon from 1861 to 1864; in Illinois Female College from 1865 to 1871; principal of the Richview public schools for six years; assistant in Mount Vernon, Ill., high school one year. Received the degree of A. M. from the Illinois Wesleyan in 1876. Elected to the chair of geography in the Southern Illinois Normal in 1878, which position she efficiently filled till a change in the administration of state affairs brought about many changes in the Board of Trustees and Faculty in 1893. She retired in June of that year. Miss Finley was active in the faculty and every good work.

MARY ALICE RAYMOND—Born in San Francisco, Cal., September 26, 1856. Educated in the public schools of St. Louis and Lebanon, and in McKendree College, where she graduated in 1873. Taught in the public schools from the lower grades to the high school of Mt. Vernon from 1874 to 1882, when she resigned to accept the position of teacher of writing and drawing in the Southern Illinois Normal. This position she filled acceptably till she resigned in 1884. Married D. B. Parkinson July 30, the same year, in whose home she contintinues to reign queen.

JOHN BENGEL, 1883-1886.—From the first there was a demand for instruction in the modern languages; this demand had been met by several of the teachers of other departments, especially by Prof. Granville F. Foster, who retired in June, 1883. Mr. Bengel was elected to the chair of modern languages soon afterward. He began his work the term in which the original building was destroyed by fire, remained a member of the faculty while in the temporary building, and closed his connection with the school the June following the opening of the present main building. He died in St. Louis in the summer of 1886.

CHARLES HARRIS, A. M., 1886-1888.—Successor to Mr. Bengel. Born in Edwards county, Ill. Educated in the home school, and in Oberlin College. After serving two years as teacher of French and German in the Normal he desired to prosecute his studies still further. This led him to resign. Since then he has been the author of several text-books in German.

MRS. CLARA B. WAY, 1890-1894.—Maiden name French. After many years of successful teaching in Mt.

Vernon and Nashville, Ill., she was called to the chair of Latin and Greek made vacant by the resignation of C. W. Jerome in 1890. She was characterized by her strict devotion to duty and high regard for the proper influence of the teacher upon the life of the student. Her sterling, womanly qualities rendered her one of the most valuable members of the corps of instructors in the institution. She now teaches in the high school of Cairo, where her services are highly prized.

ANN C. ANDERSON, 1886-1893.—Upon the resignation of Miss Alice Krysher in June of 1886, Miss Anderson was elected to the vacancy as principal of the Model School. She came from the principalship of the high school of Nashville, where she labored successfully for several years. She brought a new life to the department and inaugurated a number of new features, especially that of special teaching of music in the lower grades. With Miss Anderson began the very attractive closing exercises of the department as a part of commencement week. She resigned in 1893 to accept a position in the River Falls Normal School of Wisconsin.

JOHN M. PIERCE, A. M., 1892-1894.—Born in Oakville, Ill., December 21, 1859; son of a physician; educated in the home school and the Southern Illinois Normal University, where he entered September 11, 1876, remained several years. Afterwards attended Washington and Johns Hopkins and Harvard Universities; elected to the chair of German and Physical Training in the Southern Normal in 1892, remained two years, when he returned to Harvard to continue his studies in philosophy. At present is associated with E. O. Vaile in the publication of "Intelligence" and "News Current."

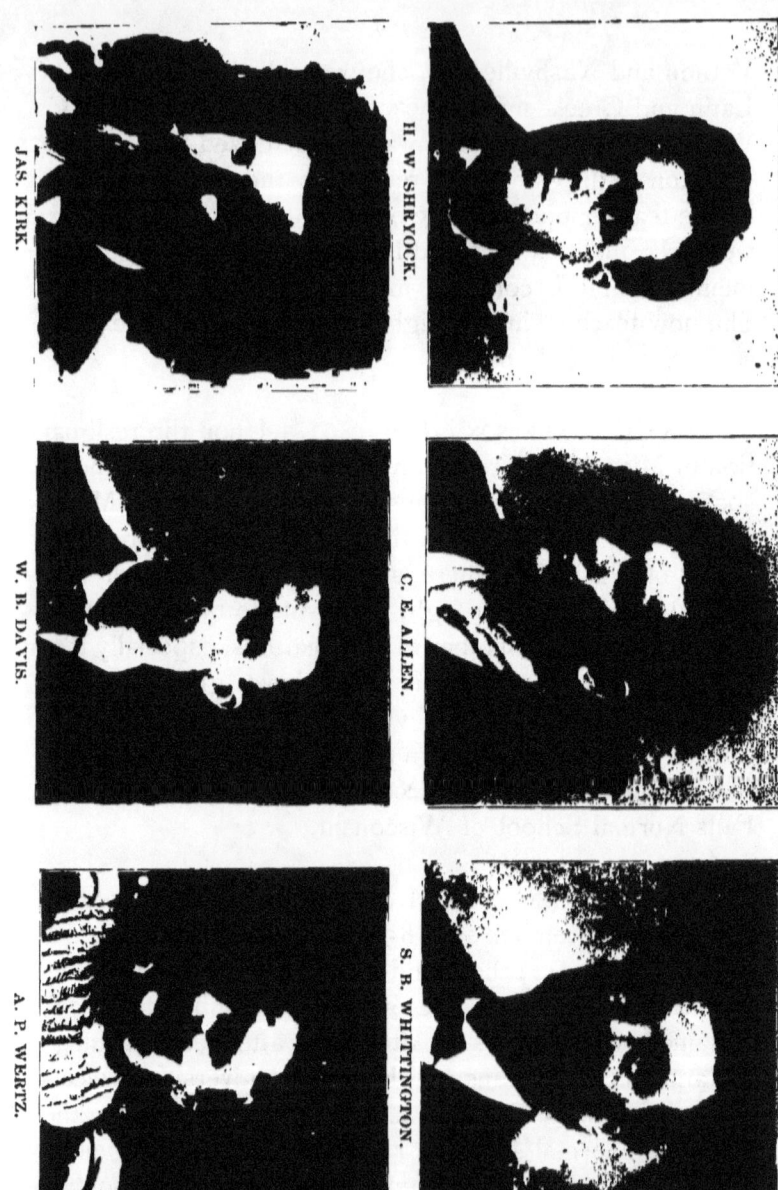

**LIBRARY
OF THE
UNIVERSITY OF ILLINOIS**

THEDA GILDEMEISTER, 1893-1897.—Upon the resignation of Miss Anderson, Miss Gildermeister was elected as principal of the first six grades of the practice school. She had for several years labored in the public schools of Hillsboro subsequent to her graduation from the Illinois State Normal. The department made marked progress under her administration, due in no small degree to the aid of an assistant which for the first time was provided. She now occupies a similar position in the State Normal at Winona, Minn.

IRENE FENGUSON, 1893-1897.—Miss Ferguson came to assist in the Practice School. Had been engaged for several years in the public schools of Hillsboro. The children in the Practice School will never forget her motherly care and thoughtful consideration of their wants. The value of her services has established the need of two teachers in charge of the first six grades. Her successor is Miss Parks, whose appointment is noted elsewhere.

PROF. SAMUEL M. INGLIS, 1883-1894.—The above former member of the Faculty filled a unique place in the institution in that he, in addition to being a teacher, was, prior to that relation, a member of the Board of Trustees, having been appointed by Governor Cullom to succeed Hon. L. M. Phillips, who died in December, 1880. Prof. Inglis served as Trustee till the expiration of the term, March 25, 1883, and later a member ex-officio. He was elected to the chair of Mathematics the same year of 1883, and served till his election to the Superintendency of Public Instruction in 1894. This position he ably filled till he was called to his reward in the better life in May, 1898. The subject of this sketch is entitled to more than a passing notice in this connection. He was regarded as an active and wise counselor in the deliberations of the Board of Trustees, ever ready to further any movement that looked toward the best interest of the institution. Having been actively engaged in the public school work for fifteen or more years, he was familiar with the needs of teachers, and was in close sympathy with the work of the different departments of the Normal.

As a member of the Faculty he was an untiring worker, an enthusiastic and inspiring teacher, and a lover of children and ambitious youth; ever on the alert to render timely service to the struggling student. His buoyant spirit served as a stimulus to his associates in spurring them to more active endeavor.

The Faculty and students were deeply interested in his candidacy for the position of State Superintendent, and recognized the compliment paid to the school when, by a large majority, he was chosen to the exalted office. They took pride in his success, and stood ready to aid him in every way possible to make his administration as popular and successful as had been his previous career as an educator.

The news of his demise cast a deep gloom over the school. But his friends rejoice that their lives came in touch with so noble a spirit, and rest in the faith that he now enjoys the rich reward that awaits the faithful and devoted laborer in the vineyard of the Master.

HANS BALLIN, a native of Germany, graduated from the High School at sixteen, and came to America at seventeen. He taught at Erie, Pa., and Sandusky, O., coming to the Normal in 1894, and remaining in charge of the gymnasium two years. He is now teaching at Little Rock, Ark.

ARISTA BURTON graduated in the class of '77, and taught in a number of High Schools in this state. She was elected to the chair of History in 1893, holding that position four years. She is now teaching at Colorado Springs, Col. (See "History of the Alumni.")

MILITARY DEPARTMENT.

CAPT. THOS. J. SPENCER, 1877-1880.—Detailed by the War Department to organize a military department in the Southern Illinois Normal in the summer of 1877. Born August 2, 1842. Educated in native city, McKendree College, and at the University of Michigan. While at the latter school he entered the Union Army May 28, 1861. Participated in the first battle of the war, June 11, 1861, at Rich Mountain, W. Va. Commissioned second lieutenant by President Lincoln August 21, 1862. Served on the staffs of Generals Rosecrans, G. H. Thomas, W. B. Hazen, M. L. Smith and Wm. T. Sherman. Participated in twenty-two general engagements and served a term in Libby, Chattanooga, Knoxville and Lynchburg prisons.

LIEUT. HUGH T. REED, 1880-1883.—Born August 17, 1852, in Richmond, Ind. Attended the public schools of that city and also a private school of same place. Entered the University of Michigan September, 1868, and remained one year, when he entered the military academy at West Point, July 1, 1869. Graduated June 13, 1873, and appointed second lieutenant. Promoted to first lieutenant July 1, 1879. Is the author of several valuable books on military science, which are used quite extensively by the government.

LIEUT. CHARLES G. STARR, 1883-1886.—Born in

Kankakee, Ill., February 25, 1857. Early education received in Kankakee, Westbrook Seminary at New Portland, Maine. Entered West Point Military Academy June 1, 1874, from the Eighth District of Illinois, graduated June 14, 1878, and appointed second lieutenant June 28. Served with honor for several years on the frontier. Married Niss Ellen A. Norton, October 13, 1881, in San Antonio, Tex. Detailed to the Military Department of the Southern Illinois Normal University, March 8, 1883. Promoted to first lieutenant September 20, 1883. At the expiration of his detail he returned to his regiment.

LIEUT. JAMES F. BELL, 1886–1889.—Capt. Spencer was the first detailed officer placed in charge of the Military Department. Lieutenant Bell was the last. However, the equipment was allowed to remain one year longer and under the management of Mr. George V. Buchanan. Lieutenant Bell was progressive in spirit and added much to the society interests of Carbondale. Because of meritorious conduct he was promoted from time to time. In the late war he was made major because of active and efficient service in the Philippine Islands, an account of which was given in many of the magazines and papers. Since the equipment for regular gymnasium work there is less demand for the Military Department, but it served an excellent purpose at the time of its existence.

PRESENT FACULTY.

The anniversary exerciss gave prominence to the early history of the institution, in all of which MISS MARTHA BUCK was an important factor. Receiving her education at Chicago and Peoria, Miss Buck spent nine years.

in public school work in Illinois before accepting the position which she now occupies in the Southern Illinois Normal. Though thoroughly progressive in her ideas along educational lines, her successful service of a quarter of a century gives to the Faculty and institution an element of conservatism that is that is essential to the stability of any institution of learning. Aside from Dr. Parkinson, Miss Buck is the only member of the present Faculty who has been connected with the Normal from its beginning.

Another veteran whom the friends of the Southern Normal delight to honor is Mr. GEORGE H. FRENCH, who has been a member of the Faculty since 1877. A normal school education in the state of New York, together with several years' experience as superintendent and college teacher of science, prepared him for the successful work which he has done during the past twenty-two years.

The work of the Department of Drawing has for the past fourteen years been in the hands of Miss MATILDA N. SALTER. Miss Salter was educated at the Bettie Stuart Institute, Springfield, Ill., and at the Cooper Institute of Art, New York. Her superior talent and excellent training in art and drawing, together with one year's successful experience as assistant principal of the Chester High School, led to her election to her present position, which she holds with credit to herself and with honor to the institution.

GEO. W. SMITH, M. A. (Blackburn University 1893), came to the Normal in 1890, having had an experience of twelve years in the public school work of the state. Possibly because of this experience as country school teacher, High School principal and city superintendent, Mr. Smith is more closely in touch with the work of the public schools than most of the members of the Faculty. After serving for seven years as training teacher in the grammar grades of the Practice School, he was made head of the Department of History and Geography, which position he now fills.

SAMUEL B. WHITTINGTON was educated at Ewing College and at Danville, Indiana. He was superintendent of the Benton, Ill., schools four years; three years at Ava, Ill., and two years at Mt. Vernon, Ill. In 1893 he came to this school as assistant in Mathematics. In 1896 he was made head of the department of Physical Training, and since 1897 has given his entire attention to this work. Mr. Whittington had completed a course in the Milwaukee Normal School for physical training, and to his efforts and superior ability is due the fact that this department is one of the most popular and successful in the Normal.

SAMUEL E. HARWOOD began his career as teacher in a log school-house three miles north of Carbondale. He afterwards taught in the public schools of Carbondale, and was, for eleven years, engaged in the public school work in Indiana, being superintendent of the Spencer and Attica schools. In 1893 he was appointed head of the department of Mathematics of the Southern Illinois Normal, which position he holds at the present time. Mr. Harwood is a graduate of the Terre Haute Normal, and of Indiana University, from which institution, in 1892, he obtained his M. A. He is the author of "Notes on Method in Arithmetic," and has contributed largely to educational journals. Himself a man of superior education, he stands for thorough and scholarly work in the institution.

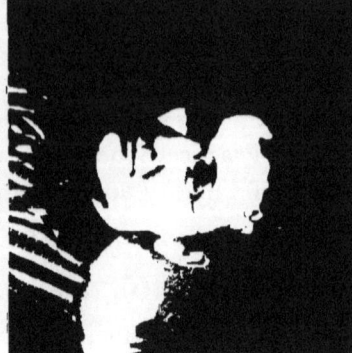

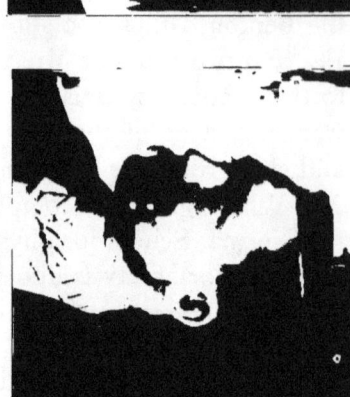

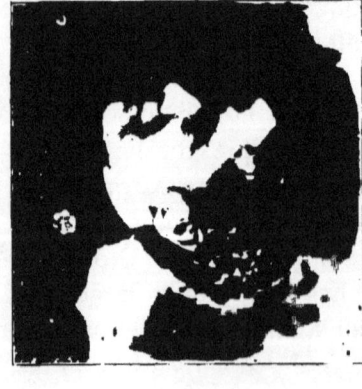

**LIBRARY
OF THE
UNIVERSITY OF ILLINOIS**

CARLOS EBEN ALLEN, chair of languages, graduated from the classic course at Carleton College, Northfield, Minn., in 1894. In 1893-4 he was tutor in Latin at the Northfield Academy. In the same year of his graduation at Carleton College, he was elected to the chair of languages Southern Illinois Normal University. This position he has since held with entire satisfaction.

HENRY W. SHRYOCK was graduated from the High School at Olney, Ill. After one year of post-graduate work there he was elected principal, which position he held for eleven years. During this time he obtained his degree of Ph. B. from the Illinois Wesleyan. In 1894 he was elected to the chair of Literature and Elocution in this institution, successor to Mr. S. M. Inglis. In 1897 hs was made Vice-President and Registrar. Mr. Shryock is one of the most popular teachers of the Normal, and is known throughout the southern portion of the state as a lecturer of ability.

JAMES KIRK prepared for college in Washington Seminary. In 1871 he was graduated from Eureka College, and in 1874 received the degree of A. M. from the same institution. He has taught in country schools, in Eureka College, has been Superintendent of Public Schools of Woodford county, and of Washburn, Minonk and Pekin, Ill., and Assistant State Superintendent of Public Instruction. In 1895 he was elected Superintendent of the Training Department of the Southern Illinois Normal. Having seen service in so many departments of education, Mr. Kirk is peculiarly fitted for his work, and is, perhaps, more widely known among school men than any other member of the Faculty.

JAMES H. BROWNLEE was graduated in 1870 from the

classical course of McKendree College, Lebanon, Illinois, and a few years later received from his Alma Mater an M. A. For eleven years he occupied the chair of Elocution and Literature in the Southern Illinois State Normal. Mr. Brownlee has become so well and favorably known throughout the state as a teacher and elocutionist that this spring, 1899, he was elected by the Board of the Charleston Normal to fill a chair in that institution. This position, much to the regret of his many friends in this part of the state, Mr. Brownlee has decided to accept.

MISS ADDA P. WERTZ received her education at Bloomington, Ill., and at the University of Minnesota. She held responsible positions as teacher and supervisor in Bloomington for twelve years. She spent five years in Minneapolis as supervising principal, and received her training there as a primary teacher under Sarah L. Arnold, now of Boston. In 1896 she entered the Southern Illinois Normal University as student of Pedagogy, and in 1897 was made principal of Primary School and training teacher of the first six grades of the Practice School. Miss Wertz is now one of the critic teachers in the training department.

ELIZABETH PARKS is an alumnus of the Southern Illinois State Normal, a member of the class of '89. After graduation she taught one year at Coulterville, and four years at Du Quoin. In 1897 she was elected to a position in the Southern Normal. She is now one of the critic teachers in the training department, where she has done excellent work with the practice teachers as well as the pupils in the Model School.

WASHINGTON BEATY DAVIS, A. M., was graduated from Wabash College, Crawfordsville, Ind, 1880, from the classical course. He was principal at Friendsville two years, Superintendent at Fairfield six years, and Superintendent at Nokomis three years. For five years he was principal of the Preparatory School and occupied the chair of History at Blackburn University, Carlinville, Ill., and Superintendent at Pittsfield, Ill., two years. In 1897 he came to the Southern Normal as principal of the Grammar Department, and has since been appointed to fill the chair of Science. Mr. Davis is best known among teachers for his successful institute work which he has done in all parts of the state.

FRANK H. COLYER, A. B., is an alumnus of the Southern Normal, a member of the class of '89. He received his degree of A. B. from Indiana University, and has attended Chicago University one year. He was Superintendent at Brown's and Albion, Ill., and at Paoli, Ind. He was elected assistant in Geography and History in the Southern Illinois Normal University in 1897. Being a university graduate and an alumnus of this institution, Mr. Colyer is looked upon as a strong man, with superior training. His work in General History is especially good.

MARY M. MCNEILL was graduated from Almira College, at Greenville, Ill. She received her musical education from private tutors in St. Louis and at the College of Music in Cincinnati. After doing studio work as a teacher of Music, she was called to the chair of Instrumental Music at the Southern Illinois Normal University in 1897.

H. J. ALVIS, another graduate of the Normal (1898) to be called to a position in his Alma Mater, has, during the past year, been an assistant in Latin and Mathematics. In the coming year he will be training teacher in charge of the grammar grades of the Practice School.

Mr. Alvis has taught several years in the public schools of the state, and was, at the time of his election here, Principal of the High School at Nashville, Ill. Considering his length of service in the Normal, a more popular teacher can, perhaps, not be found in the Faculty.

Miss Minnie J. Fryar (class of '86, S. I. N. U.) taught in Anna, Carbondale, and Clinton, Iowa, six years in all. In 1892 she was elected Librarian at her Alma Mater, which position she has since held with credit, having indexed the Library according to the modern Dewey system. She has done other efficient work.

Miss Augusta McKinney was educated at the Southern Illinois Normal University. She taught eight years in the public schools of Carbondale, after which she worked with Meyer Brothers Drug Co., St. Louis, until she came here in the summer of 1897 as stenographer and clerical assistant.

**LIBRARY
OF THE
UNIVERSITY OF ILLINOIS**

1. George C. Ross, '76.
2. Mary Wright, '76.
3. James H. England, '77.
4. William H. Warder, '77.
5. Delia Caldwell, M. D., '78.
6. Charles E. Evans, '78.
7. Sarah Jackson Kimmel, '78.
8. John T. McAnally, M. D. '78.
9. Mary McAnally Moss, 78.
10. Andrew C. Burnett, '79.
11. Ida M. McCreery, '79.
12. Lizzie Sheppard Miller, '80.
13. Gertrude Warder Michelet,'80
14. William F. Hughes, '81.
15. Henry W. Karraker, '81.
16. John W. Lorenz, '81.
17. Oscar S. Marshall, '81.
18. Edwyad I. Ward, '81.
19. Wezetta Atkins Parkinso
20. Lizzie Deardorf DeMoss,
21. Walter J. Ennison, '82.
22. Adella Goodall Mitchell,
23. Alice Krysher Livingston
24. Albert E. Mead, '82.
25. John W. Wood, '82.

Sketches of Alumni.

AT a late date it was decided to write to each member of the Alumni Association to secure facts from which short biographical sketches might be written. We give below sketches of all from whom we have heard up to time for going to press. We regret that space does not allow a lengthy biography of each, and that all have not been heard from, but we feel sure that these brief notices will be of interest to the Alumni Association and friends of the school:

Annie R. Alexander, '91, was born in Indiana, but moved to Illinois when quite young. Since graduation she has taught two years in the southern part of Illinois, one in Flora, and four in Harvey.

R. M. Allen, '87, entered railway service in 1889, since which time he has held various responsible railway positions. He is now Assistant General Passenger Agent of the Louisville, Evansville & St. Louis Consolidated Railroad, with headquarters at St. Louis, Mo.

Margaret Gordon Anderson, '95, was born in Carbondale and graduated from the public school in '91, taught two years before completing the course in the Normal, and since that time taught three years in Flora, Ill., and one as Principal of the West Side School in Carbondale, which position she now retains.

Wezette Atkins Parkinson, '82, was valedictorian of of her class. She was married to Chas. W. Parkinson in 1883, and spent eight years in the west. Returning to Illinois in 1891, she taught three years with her husband in Vandalia. The past five years they have resided in Murphysboro. They are soon to make their home in Edwardsville, where Mr. Parkinson goes next year to superintend the schools.

R. May Baker, '95, of Cottage Home, Ill., has taught two and one-half years near her home since graduation.

Ola Baughman Bainum, '95, was born near Olney, Ill., and graduated from the High School of that place in '93. She taught one year before entering the Normal, and was married shortly after graduation to Mr. George Bainum, of Flora, Ill., which place is now her home.

James W. Barrow, '98, is a native of Jackson county. He attended the village school at Campbell Hill, and then entered the Southern Illinois Normal University, graduating in 1898. He taught in McLeansboro as Principal of the High School last year, and has been chosen as Superintendent for the coming year.

Rachel Jane Barter, '97, a farmer's daughter from Williamson county, completed the English-Latin course. She has taught three years in the higher grades of the schools of Galatia, Mt. Vernon and Golconda.

Josie Barton Goodnow, '95, was born in Carbondale, and educated in the public school and the Normal. She taught two years after graduation in Bunker Hill, Ill. She was was married Sept. 28, 1898, to Mr. Fred Clinton Goodnow, of Salem, Ill., and now lives in that city.

Anson L. Bliss, '92, was born near Mt. Vernon, Ill. He attended school at home, at Ewing College, taught at home, started an academy in the Choctaw Nation, and taught in Gainesville, Texas, before graduating from the Normal. He graduated from Austin College in '95 with the degree of A. B. He was Superintendent of the Cobden High School three years when he resigned to superintend the Anna High School, which position he now holds.

Cincinnatus Boomer, '96, has been teaching in Johnson county since graduation. Because of ill health he could not complete last year's school term.

A. Sherman Boucher, '98, a Jackson county farmer's son, entered the Normal at eighteen. He taught three terms in the rural schools, and two at Murphysboro. Last year he was High School Principal at Metropolis, and next year will fill the same position at Edwardsville.

Frank Leslie Boyd, '91, is a native of Indiana. He has taught school twenty-one years in Illinois, Kansas and Colorado. Was Superintendent of Carbondale Public Schools five years. Is now a lumber dealer in Boulder, Colorado.

Mary Buchanan, '84, was born in Wabash county, Ill. Graduated from the Mt. Carmel High School, then entered the Southern Illinois Normal University and remained three years. She has since taught seven years, and worked for the Central School Journal of Missouri two years. The last three years she has spent in Carbondale with her mother.

Clara J. Buchanan Merrimon, '84, was born in Wabash county, Ill. She graduated from the Mt. Carmel High School in '81, then attended the Southern Illinois Normal University three years. She taught two years, then married Mr. H. Merrimon in 1896. She now lives on a farm near Elizabethtown, and is the mother of four boys and two girls.

Nina Buchanan, '98, has been teaching during the

year 1898-99 at Vincennes, Ind. She will teach next year at Lawrenceville, Ill., as Principal of the High School.

A. C. Burnett, '79, was born in Randolph county, Ill. He attended the S. I. N. U. for four years, then located in Lamar, Mo.; married Miss Frank in 1881, and began the practice of law in 1884. He has served as prosecuting attorney two terms; also been cashier of First National Bank of Lamar three years.

Joseph B. Bundy, '92, was born in Saline county, Ill., entered the Southern Normal in 1884, taught four years in the rural schools of Jackson county; two years as Principal of the East Side School at Murphysboro; six years as Superintendent of the city schools of Nashville, Ill. Now with the Ayer & Lord Tie Co.

May Cleland, '87, taught in the schools of Cook county the four years after graduation, then entered the Illinois Training School for Nurses and was graduated in 1896. Since that time she has followed her profession in Evanston, except a few months of last year, when she was sent as an army nurse to Camp Wikoff, Montauk.

Clara Cleland Strong, '87, went to Chicago after graduation and taught one year in Cook county. On July 5, 1888, she was married to Mr. J. W. Strong, of Wheeling, Cook county, Ill. She now lives in Evanston, Ill., 1108 Asbury avenue.

David J. Cowan, '87, has, since graduation, divided his time between teaching and the practice of law. Much of his time has been spent in the west. He was in the notorious race for land in the Cherokee Strip on the 16th of September, 1893. Since 1895 he has been in Vienna, Ill., practicing law.

Arthur G. Cross, '97, was reared on a farm near

1. Frank M. Alexander, '83.
2. Alice Buckley Alexander, '83.
3. Daniel B. Fager, '83.
4. Fannie Aikman Kimmel, '84.
5. Clara Buchanan Merrimon, '84
6. George V. Buchanan, '84.
7. Mary Buchanan, '84.
8. Anna Burket, '84.
9. Mary B. Duff, '84.
10. Joseph B. Gill, '84.
11. John H. Jenkins, '84.
12. Richard T. Lightfoot, '84.
13. Carrie Ridenhower Mount, '84
14. Maud Thomas, '84.
15. Ada Dunaway Caldwell, '85.
16. William R. Fringer, '85.
17. Mary Robarts Ogden, '85.
18. Sarah Allen Crenshaw, '86.
19. Minnie Fryar, '86.
20. Alexander H. Fulton, '86.
21. Ella Hundley Andrews, '86.
22. Carrie Loomis McCreery, '86
23. Fannie McAnally Fager, '86.
24. Louella Nichols Irwin, '86.
25. Edgar L. Storment, '86.
26. Cora Williams, '86.

**LIBRARY
OF THE
UNIVERSITY OF ILLINOIS**

Campbell Hill. At the age of eighteen he taught school in Campbell Hill, and entered the Normal the following spring.

Mary E. Davis Snyder, '92, was born in Centralia, Ill., where she graduated from the High School in 1889. Immediately after graduating from the Normal she was married to Mr. Arthur J. Snyder. She has continued the study of botany, and collected specimens in Utah in 1893. Her present home is Belvidere, Ill.

Lizzie Deardorff DeMoss, '82, was born near Cobden, Ill. She taught six years after graduation in Illinois and Kansas, married Mr. H. DeMoss in 1891, and has since lived in Ballard, Washington.

Ada Dunaway Caldwell, '85, attended school at Lasell Seminary, Auburndale, Mass., the year after graduation; afterwards spent several months traveling in Europe. In 1894 she was married to Andrew S. Caldwell at Carbondale, Ill., where she is now living with her husband and small son of three years.

Viola Vosburg Cundiff Rendleman, '96, was born in Cairo, Ill., and graduated from the Cairo High School. She has taught school one year each in Nebraska and Arkansas, and three years in Illinois. She was married to Dr. Rendleman, of Cairo, in January of 1899.

Jacob T. Ellis, '94, of Mt. Vernon, first entered the Normal in 1884. He taught several years before graduating, and four since as Superintendent of the Greenville schools; also one as Superintendent of the Mt. Vernon schools, which position he now holds. He was married in 1895 to Miss Beulah Nowland, a former student. He is now taking special work in the Chicago University.

John W. Emmerson, '92, was born and raised near

Albion, Ill. He has taught since graduation in Marion, Mt. Vernon, Nashville and Albion, and is re-elected Superintendent of the Albion High School. In 1896 he received a life state certificate. In 1897 he was married to Miss Grettie Hitchcock.

James H. England, '77, was born in Tennessee. Removed to Illinois in 1863; was married to Miss Coral Cardon in August, 1874. He has spent twenty-five years in the school-room.

W. J. Ennison, '82, began the study of law after graduation, and in 1884 began practicing in Chicago. Since 1892 he has spent his time on an invention in the machine line, and is now working in an office at Hartford, Connecticut.

Guy Everett Etherton, '96, taught in the public schools of the state two years. He attended Oberlin College three terms, and graduated from the Chicago Theological Seminary in 1899. He is now pastor of the Congregational Church at Argentine, Kansas.

Wm. Alonzo Etherton, '97, has had charge of the schools at Carterville, Ill., since his graduation. This fall he begins a course in Architectural Engineering at the University of Illinois.

D. B. Fager, '83, began teaching when but a youth. His first experience dates back to 1875. Since graduation he has taught continuously and successfully. Since 1895 he has been City Superintendent of the Salem Public Schools. On July 7, 1887, he was married to Miss Fannie D. McAnally, class of '86.

Minnie R. Flint, '96, was born in Sparta, Ill., and attended various village schools in Illinois. Since graduation she has taught one year in East St. Louis, and one year in Belleville High School.

William R. Fringer, '86, entered the Medical Department of the Northwestern University of Chicago soon after graduating from the Normal, and completed the course there in 1888. While practicing general medicine and surgery with his father in Tunnel Hill, Ill., he spent some time both in Chicago and New York City devoting himself to the special study of the eye. He located in Rockford, Ill., in 1892, where his practice is limited to the diseases of the eye. He will spend this summer in Europe.

Alexander H. Fulton, '86, was born and raised in Marion county, Ill. He has taught seventeen years in the public schools of Illinois and Arizona. In the fall of 1898 he was elected County Superintendent of Maricopa county, Arizona, and makes his home in Phœnix.

J. P. Gilbert, '96, of Jefferson county, has taught since graduation as Superintendent of City Schools in McLeansboro, and resigned to enter Chicago University in the fall of 1899.

Joseph B. Gill, '84, was educated in the common schools, the Christian Brothers College, of St. Louis, and the S. I. N. U. He graduated from the law school at Ann Arbor in 1893. He was married to Miss Pearl Hall in 1893. He has engaged in newspaper work, been Lieutenant Governor, also a member of the State Board of Arbitration since graduation. He now resides in San Bernardino, Cal., with his wife and one child.

Albin Z. Glick, '87, was born in Fairfield couny, O., and removed with his parents to Illinois when small. He was educated in the common schools and the Normal.

He has taught seven years. He is now Deputy of Modern Woodmen of America. His home is in Carbondale.

Kate Gracia Hackney Rogers, '90, was born near Zanesville, Ill., where she received her early education and did her first teaching. After graduatisn she taught two years, then married Frederick O. Rogers, of Waggoner. and now lives on a farm near that city.

May Keeney Hayes, '97, was born in DesMoines, Iowa, and received her early education there. She entered the Normal in '91, and, since graduating, has done two years' work in the Prang Normal Art Course.

Ada Hickam Wood, '88, was born in Carbondale and educated in the public schools and the Normal. She taught three years, then married Mr. G. W. Wood, and with him entered the drug business. She is now located in Beechwood, is a registered apprentice, and is working to become a druggist.

Adda Hord, '91, has, since leaving school, spent seven years teaching in the schools of Flora, Makanda and Cobden. Her home is now at Murphysboro.

Lily M. Houts, '83, has, since leaving the Normal. taught four years. She was engaged in Chicago with work connected with the Religious Congresses during the World's Fair year, and afterwards became a stenographer in the Fort Dearborn National Bank, where she is still employed.

Margaret Huggins, '98, of Swanwick, Perry county, completed the four years course in the Sparta High School in 1892. She afterwards taught three years in the schools of Pinckneyville. She taught the past year in Lemhi, Idaho, and will teach during the year 1899–1900 at Salmon, Idaho.

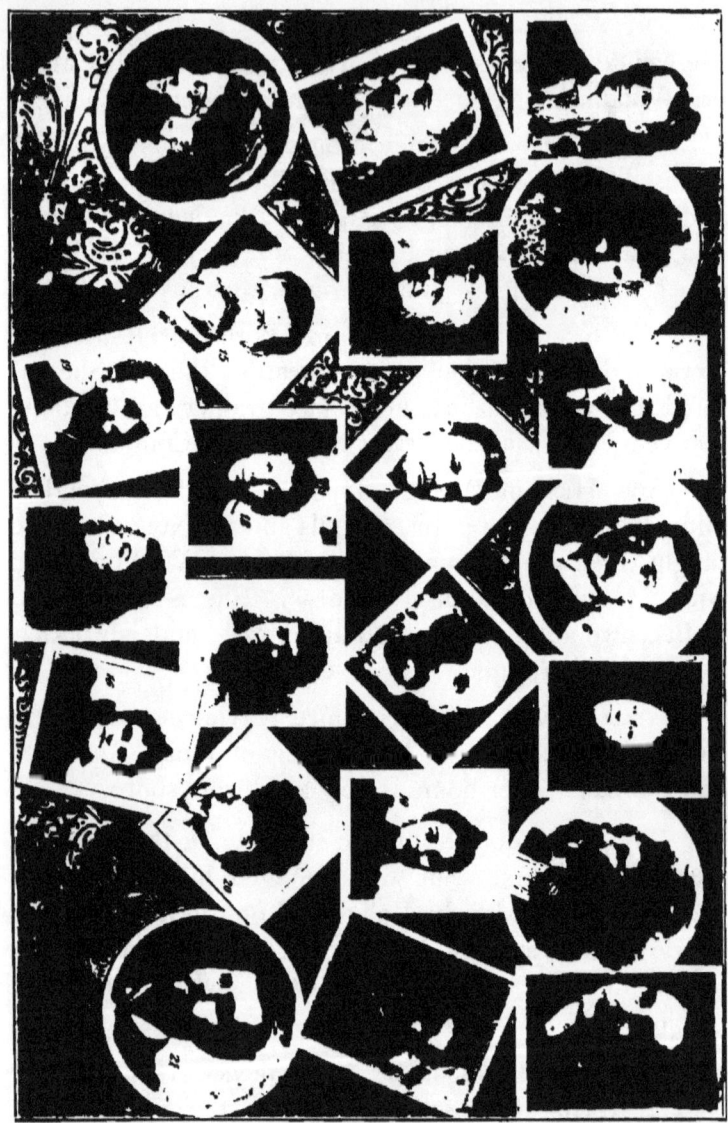

1. Robert M. Allen, '87.
2. Carrie Blair, '87.
3. Rockwell Bryden, '87.
4. May Cleland, '87.
5. David J. Cowan, '87.
6. Albin Z. Glick, '87.
7. Samuel H. Goodall, '87.
8. Nannie Hundley, '87.
9. James H. Kirkpatrick, '87.
10. Bertha Lawrence, '87.
11. Louise E. Phillips, '87.
12. Charles H. Ripley, '87.
13. Luther T. Scott, '87.
14. Minnie Tait Ripley, '87.
15. Steuben D. Wham, '87.
16. Ada Hickam Wood, '88.
17. Callie Johnson, '88.
18. Mary E. Leary, '88.
19. William A. Reef, '88.
20. Kate E. Richards Stewart, '88
21. Frank E. Trobaugh, M.D., '88
22. Maggie Wham Wiley, '88.

**LIBRARY
OF THE
UNIVERSITY OF ILLINOIS**

William F. Hughes, '81, was born in West Virginia; came to Illinois in 1857; lived near Carbondale, and after graduation took a four years course in Science and Literature in New York. He taught a number of years, then was appointed County Surveyor in 1894. He is a first-class surveyor, and is called upon to settle disputes and make difficult surveys.

Nannie Hundley, '87, has been teaching in graded school work since graduation. At present she is in Marion, Ill., where she has taught three years in the High School.

Sarah E. Jackson Kimmell, '78, was born near Du Quoin, Ill.; attended the High School there four years, and then entered the S. I. N. U., its first term. She was married to Mr. H. H. Kimmell in 1882; lives on a farm near Du Quoin. She is the mother of one boy.

Harriet E. Jenkins, '94, of Elkville, Ill., has taught four years since graduating—two in Elkville, one in Mt. Vernon, and one in Greenville, Ill.

David Oscar Jones, '95, was born in Franklin county. He began teaching when twenty years of age, then attended school at Ewing, and later at the Normal. Since graduating he has taught each year, and is now Principal of the De Soto, Ill., schools. He married Miss Cora Nichols in March, 1896.

Henry W. Karraker, '81, taught fifteen terms after graduation; served two and one-half years as cashier in the Bank of Jonesboro; he lives on a farm west of Dongola. In 1893 he was ordained to the ministry in the Missionary Baptist Church, and is doing much pastoral work.

I. O. Karraker, '96, of Union county, attended Union Academy at Anna two years. After graduation he taught in Marion, Ill., as Principal of the High School one year, and as Superintendent one year, resigning the latter position to become cashier in the Jonesboro Bank.

Lincoln S. Kell, '94, of Salem, Ill., has devoted his time to farming since graduation, and has made a success of his work.

Lucy Kell, '94, has taught five years, the last three at Kell, Ill.

Belle Kimmel, '83, has taught in Illinois, Idaho and California since graduation. She is now at her home in Elkville, Ill., where she enjoys life and is kept busy.

Jas. T. Kirk, '97, was born in Eureka, Ill., and attended school at Eureka, Pekin and Springfield, completing the four years' High School course at the latter place. Since graduation he has taught one year and attended Eureka College one year.

Jas. H. Kirkpatrick, '87, went to Puget Sound in the fall of 1887, and has since been so well pleased with the far west that he has not returned to his native state. He has taught ten years and now owns a fine farm overlooking the Gulf of Georgia, with beautiful mountain scenery and picturesque views on every hand.

Uriah Kissinger, '97, has, since his graduation from the Normal, been Principal of the schools of Elkhart, Ill.

Mary G. Lansden, '90, graduated from the Cairo High School in '87, then entered the S. I. N. U. Since graduation she has taught in Shawneetown, Anna and the public schools of Chicago. She now teaches seventh grade in one of the newest and best equipped schools of Chicago.

Mary E. Leary, '88, taught six years in the public schools of Illinois after graduating, and in '93 took a position in the institution for the education of the deaf and dumb, Jacksonville, Ill. After five years' work there she was offered the position of head teacher of the Oral Department of the Iowa School for the Deaf at Council Bluffs, where she is now teaching.

J. W. Lindley, '92, was born in Crawford county. He taught one year after graduation, then began the study of law under G. T. Bradberry, of Robinson, Ill. He was admitted to practice in 1894, and removed to Sullivan, Ind., where he has an office and is succeeding in his practice.

David W. Lindsay, '88, was born in Richland county, Ill. He taught eight years before graduating, and for six years after graduating in the S. I. N. U. was Superintendent of the Greenville High School. In 1894 he went to California and took charge of the Porterville schools. In 1898 he graduated from the Leland Stanford University, and was again called to Porterville, where he still teaches.

Ada Lingenfelter, '93, taught four years before graduating, and one year after. In September, 1895, she entered the Chicago Training School for Home and Foreign Missions. She is now engaged in active deaconess work for the Lincoln Street Church, aid to Miss Jefferson, Superintendent of Deaconess Home.

John W. Lorenz, '81, was born near Highland, Ill., taught two years successfully, then attended S. I. N. U. three years. After graduation he taught four years in Highland. Was married to Miss Sophia A. Wehrly in 1882. In 1885 he became a druggist, and in 1887 graduated from the National Institute of Pharmacy at Chicago, and in 1895 received the degree of Doctor of Medicine.

Leah McGahey, '96, of Olnny, has taught one year at Arthur, Ill., one year in the fourth grade in Olney, and one as Second Assistant Principal of the Olney High School.

John D. McMeen, '89, was born and raised in Jefferson county, Ill. After completing the course in the Normal he graduated from Draughn's Practical Business College in Texarkana, Texas, in 1891, and in the Gem City Business College, Quincy, Ill., in 1892. He has taught ten years in the public schools of Illinois and Texas, and is elected Superintendent of the Lawrenceville, Ill., schools for the next school year.

Thomas S. Marshall, '81, was made assistant cashier of the Salem National Bank immediately after graduation, which position he held until 1891, when he was elected cashier. He has been a useful citizen, and is now mayor of his home city; also a member of the State Board of Agriculture from his Congressional District.

Oscar S. Marshall, '81, attended the S. I. N. U. three years; soon after graduation he entered the employ of the O. & M. Railway Company in the station at Salem, Ill. He has spent most of his time since in the employ of different railway companies, and is now station agent for the C. & C. R'y. Co. at Salem, Ill.

Lois Allyn Mason, '89, taught four years after graduation in the Murdock High School of Winchendon, Mass. In 1893 she was married to Mr. Dwignt L. Mason. She is an Auxiliary Visitor of the Massachusetts State Board of Charity, and takes an active part in the Woman's Educational Club and the Woman's Board of Missions in her city.

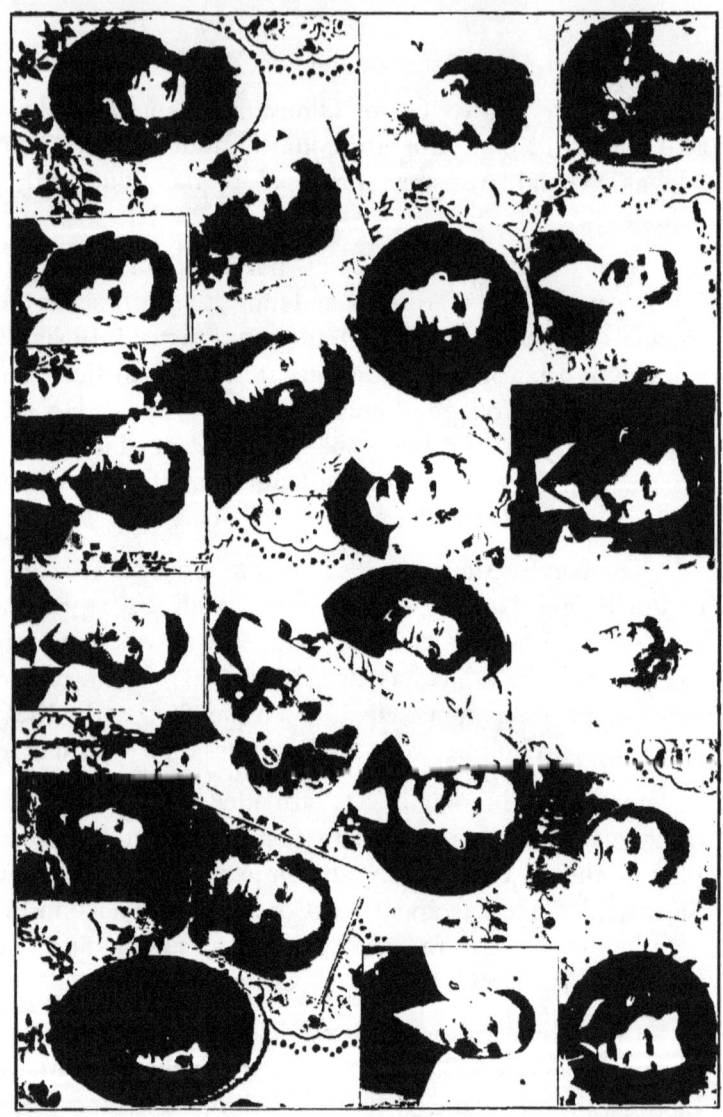

1. Lois Allyn Mason, '89.
2. Frank H. Colyer, '89.
3. John D. McMeen, '89.
4. Elizabeth Parks, '89.
5. Kate Hackney Rogers, '90.
6. Joseph E. Ramsey, '90.
7. Mabel Smith, '90,
8. Martin F. VanCleve, '90.
9. Anna R. Alexander, '91.
10. Frank L. Boyd, '91.
11. Grace L. Burket, '91.
12. James A. Freeman, '91.
13. Mary E. Hill, '91.
14. Emma Holden Ross, '91.
15. Addie Hord, '91.
16. J. Ham Lawrence, '91.
17. Maude L. Loomis, '91.
18. Elizabeth S. Peebles, '91.
19. Arthur J. Snyder, '91.
20. Theodora Sprecher, '91.
21. Robert E. Steele, '91.
22. William Whitney, '91.

**LIBRARY
OF THE
UNIVERSITY OF ILLINOIS**

Albert E. Mead, '82, taught one year, studied law. He practiced law in Blaine, Wash. In 1893 was a member of the legislature. He is now prosecuting attorney of Whatcom county, and practices law in New Whatcom City, Wash. He has aided in securing a state normal university in his own western city, which will open in September.

Louella Nichols Irwin, '86, was educated in the Carlyle Public Schools and the Southern Illinois Normal University. She taught seven years in the public schools of the state, and was married in the fall of 1895 to John G. Irwin, a prominent lawyer of Edwardsville, Ill., where she now resides.

Cora Evalyn Nichols Jones, '95, was born in Missouri and lived in Sedalia twelve years, graduating from the High School there in 1885; she removed with her parents to Pope county, Ill., where she taught three years; since graduating at the Normal she taught one year, then married her classmate, D. O. Jones, and has been occupied with home duties since.

J. Howard Ogle, '94, of Belleville, entered the Cascadilla School, New York, in the fall after graduating from the S. I. N. U. Finished the course there in 1895, and entered the Freshman Class in Electrical Engineering in Cornell University, Ithaca, N. Y. He graduated this year with the degree of Mechanical Engineer.

Elizabeth S. Peebles, '91, spent six years in the schools of Illinois and Wisconsin. She moved to Montana in 1897, and was elected County Superintendent in the fall of 1898.

R. H. Perrott, '96, was born in 1884, and has been in school work constantly with the exception of one year.

He is at present Superintendent of the Nokomis Public Schools.

Grant Peterson, '92, was educated in the Carterville public schools and the Normal. Since graduating he has devoted his time to farming near Carterville.

Louise E. Phillips, '87, entered the Normal in 1881. After finishing the couse she taught in Cairo, Ill., and later spent three years at the New England Conservatory of Music. Since 1891 she has made her home in Chicago studying and teaching music.

Lucy Haven Phillips, '97, was born in Nashville, Ill. Since graduating she has not taught school, but is teaching music in Tempe, Arizona.

Estella Ramsey, '95, of Oskaloosa, Ill., had grades certificate at fourteen. After graduating from the S. I. N. U. she taught four years, and is now serving her second term as one of the Republican State Central Committee. She is now at home on Maplewood farm, her birth-place, near Oskaloosa.

William A. Reef, '88, was born in Edwards county, Ill. He taught one year after graduating, then studied shorthand, and took a position as stenographer in Harrisburg, Ill. He went to Leadville, Col., in 1890, and for five years was official court stenographer. In 1895 he entered mercantile life, and now has a grocery store of his own, where he carries on a successful, growing business. He married Miss Nettie Melvin in 1894, and has one son, whom he hopes to educate in the S. I. N. U.

Emma Roane, '95, of Opdyke, Ill., has taught in the High Schools of Mt. Vernon, Salem and Geneseo, Ill., successively. Home duties kept her employed last year, but she will again teach in the Mt. Vernon High School the coming year.

Charles H. Ripley, '87, entered the Law School of the University of Michigan and graduated in 1889. In 1890 he was admitted to the Supreme Court in Illinois. Was married in 1892, and has since been practicing in Chicago. He is a member of the Marquette Club of Chicago, and also of the Royal Arcanum and Orator Lake View Council.

Samuel T. Robinson, '96, Saline county, was Superintendent of Schools at Ashley, Ill., two years before graduation, and has since been Superintendent at Benton three years. For next year he has the same position at Hillsboro.

Geo. C. Ross, '76, born and raised on a farm. After graduation he taught successfully several years, then turned his attention to the study of law and was graduated from Union College of Law, Northwestern University in 1881. He practiced his profession in Benton, Ill., till 1890, when he accepted a position in the law force of the Interior Department in Washington, D. C., where he has since remained.

Julia A. Sebastian, '87, has since graduation taught in the public schools of Illinois and later of Missouri. For the past six years she has held a very desirable position in the Marquette School of St. Louis, Mo. Her home is at 4227 Delmar Ave.

Andrew E. Shepherd, '98, hails from Franklin county. Beginning at the age of eighteen, he taught five terms in the rural schools. He entered the Normal in 1894. He has, since graduation, beem employed as Principal of the Grand Tower Public Schools.

Adelbert Leroy Spiller, '96, of Jackson county, is a farmer's son, and entered the Normal in 1892. He has since graduated from the Northern Illinois College of Law at Dixon.

Arthur J. Snyder, '91, was born at Farina. Since graduation he has taught at Ava, North Evanston and Belvidere. He has done special work in Entomology and Biology, being one of the organizers of the Chicago Entomological Society.

Mamie E. Songer, '93, was born in Kinmundy, Ill., where she received her early education. After graduation she taught three years, and spent her vacations traveling. She was given charge of the Normal exhibit at the World's Fair four weeks. She now lives with her parents in Kinmundy.

Minnie Tait Ripley, '87, was married in 1892 to her classmate, Chas. H. Ripley, and is now living in Chicago, making home happy for her husband and little daughter Lois, aged two years.

Edna Ozburn Thornton, '98, comes from Osage, Franklin county. She entered the Normal at fifteen, graduating in four years. She taught the following year in the public schools.

Nina Thornton, '98, of Osage, entered the Normal in 1893 at the age of fifteen, and completed the English-Latin course. She taught in 1898–1899 at Benton as Assistant Principal of the High School, and returned to that place as Principal.

Wm. Lafayette Toler, '98, is a native of Union county; entered the Normal in 1891, graduating in the English-Latin course. In the meantime he taught three years in the public schools and one year as Principal of

1. Anson L. Bliss, '92.
2. Joseph B. Bundy, '92.
3. Mary E. Davis Snyder, '92.
4. John W. Emerson, '92.
5. Charles M. Galbraith, '92.
6. Blanche Lawrence, '92.
7. John W. Lindley, '92.
8. Grant Peterson, '92.
9. Mary Wallis, '92.
10. Agnes Wham Reed, '92.
11. Dora Wham Pyatt, '92.
12. Jennie Henninger, '93.
13. Robert E. Renfro, '98.
14. Mary E. Songer, '93.
15. Sarah Whittenberg, '93.
16. Myrtle F. Woodson, '93.
17. John L. Applegath, '94.
18. May Applegath Wiswell, '91.
19. Jacob T. Ellis, '94.
20. William Troy Felts, '94.
21. Jennie Hodge Felts, '94.
22. Norman A. Jay, '94.
23. Iva Lucy Kell, '94.
24. Lincoln S. Kell, '94.
25. Eric Mohlenbrock, '94.
26. Howard J. Ogle, '94.
27. Estelle Ramsey, '94.
28. Edgar A. Smith, '94.
29. Arthur E. Williams, '94.

**LIBRARY
OF THE
UNIVERSITY OF ILLINOIS**

High School at Sandoval. Since graduating he has been Superintendent of the City Schools at Jonesboro.

Laura M. Truscott, '96, of Wayne county, attended the National Normal University at Lebanon, O. Since graduation she has taught one year each in the High Schools at Vienna and Pinckneyville.

Martin T. Van Cleve, '90, attended the S. I. N. U. two years, and was elected County Superintendent of Johnson County after graduation. Since 1896 he has been Superintendent of the Shawneetown schools.

Mary Wallis, '92, taught one year after graduating, then entered the Ohio Wesleyan University in the fall of 1893. She graduated in 1897 with the degree of B. A., and has taught since. She is re-elected as First Assistant in the Olney High School.

William Wallis, '89, has taken a college course at the Ohio Wesleyan University since leaving our Normal, receiving the degree of B. S. in June, 1894. He is now Principal of the High School In Charleston, Ill., where he has been located for the past five years.

Edward I. Ward, '81, spent seven years as teacher and Superintendent in the public schools of Southern Illinois. Was County Superintendent of schools in Perry County four years, three years a druggist and three years served as pastor of the church of Christ. Is now teaching in London, Miss.

Nellie Weller, '97, is a native of Pennsylvania. She spent her early days there, and upon moving to Carbondale entered the Normal. She taught during the past year near Murphysboro.

Agnes Wham Reed, '92, taught five years at Deland, Ill., after graduating from the S. I. N. U.

Eldora Wham Pyatt, '92, was born and raised in Marion county. She taught since graduating in Marion, Jackson and Perry county and now lives on a farm near Pyatt station.

G. D. Wham, '96, of Salem, Marion county, was Principal of the Patoka public schools two years before graduation. Since graduation he has been principal of the Olney High School, spending his vacations in Chicago University.

Margaret Wham, '88, has taught continuously since graduation. One year in the Du Quoin High School and since in the Deland schools.

S. D. Wham, '87, was born in Marion county, Ill. His early years were fraught with many hardships. He taught five years before entering the Normal. Since graduating he has been managing his farm near Cartter, Marion county, Ill. He was married in 1879.

Eugene Williams, '94, of Mt. Vernon, Ill., has taught continuously since receiving his diploma. He will possibly enter the profession of law in a short time, but is now at his home in Mt. Vernon.

Margaret Wilson, '98, graduated in the Latin course of the Cairo High School in 1895. She graduated from the Normal in the long course and accepted the Principalship of the Carlyle High School. During the coming year she will teach Latin in the Hillsboro public schools.

Below we give an alphabetical list of the Alumni from whom biographical sketches have not been received up to the time for going to press. This list also includes Alumni who are or have been members of the faculty of the S. I. N. U. Most of these have been heard from, but since their sketches appear elsewhere in the volume they were not included in the foregoing list.

Aikman, Fannie A., (Mrs. D. L. Kimmell, '84) deceased.

Alexander, F. M., '83, taught two years. Minister, Ottawa, Kan.

Allen, Sarah (Mrs. J. D. Crenshaw, '86), taught one year. Carbondale.

Alvis, Hary J., '98, professor in S. I. N. U., Carbondale.

Amon, Bertram, '97, taught one year. Deceased.

Applegath, John L. '94, taught four years. Carbondale.

Applegath, May A. (Mrs. A. Wiswell), taught four years. Carbondale.

Ayer, Philip S., '92, taught six years. Baxter Springs, Kan.

Bain, Wm. B., '83, merchant. Vienna.

Bain, John Chas., '90, lawyer. Chicago.

Barber, Florence M. (Mrs. Boyd, '86), taught two years. Chicago.

Barnes, Belle, D. A. (Mrs. H. H. Green, '77). Bloomington.

Barnum, J. A., '98.

Barr, Jessie G., '92, taught six years. Escanaba, Mich.

Baumberger, Louise (Mrs. S. M. Inglis, '88), taught seven years. Chicago.

Beesley, Alicia, '84, taught three years. Linn.

Beman, Geo. W., '91, taught one year. Clerk. Chicago.

Bennett, Frances W., '95, taught three years. Cairo.

Berkley, Helen L., '97, taught two years. Murphysboro.

Blair, Carrie, '87, taught seven years. Deceased.

Blake, Edward L., '99. Equality.

Blanchard, Guy, '91, taught one year. Merchant. Tamaroa.

Boulden, Hattie A., '97, taught one year. Fordice.

Brainard, Pearl, '99. Carbondale.

Brainard, Stuart, '99. Carbondale.

Brewster, Libbie, '99. Carbondale.

Briback, Catherine (Mrs. Hans Johnson, '88), taught eight years. Cairo.

Bridges, Mary E. (Mrs. D. L. Malone, '89), Sikeston, Mo.

Bridges, Abbie L., '97, taught two years. Cobden.

Bridges, Ella L., '97, taught two years. Carbondale.

Bridges, Rolland E., '97. Bookkeeper. Chicago.

Brown, John N., '76, taught six years.

Brown, Adella (Mrs. J. O. Ashenhurst, '86), taught nine years.

Brown, Robert, '93, taught six years. Principal. Assumption.

Bruck, Lauren L.,'80, taught seven years. Bookkeeper. Chicago.

Bryden, Margaret (Mrs. J. N. Fitch, '83), taught nine years. Cobden.

Bryden, Helen, '85, taught thirteen years. Principal. Carbondale.

Bryden, Rockwell, '87. Postal clerk. Carbondale.

Buchanan, Geo. V., '84, taught fifteen years. Superintendent schools. Sedalia, Mo.

Buckley, Alice M. (Mrs. F. M. Alexander, '83), taught two years. Ottawa, Kan.

Buckley, Ida M. (Mrs. G. W. Warner, '85), taught one year. Freeport.

Buckley, Elizabeth (Mrs. O. J. Rude, '92), taught one year. Carbondale.

Bundy, Jos. B., '92, taught six years. Manager Telephone Exchange. Carbondale.

Burge, Lloyd E., '94, taught three years. Centralia.

Burket, Anna L., '84, taught two years. Carbondale.

Burket, Grace, '91, taught five years. Carbondale.

Burkhart, Carl, '97. Merchant. Marion.

Burnett, Andrew C., '79. Lawyer. Lamar, Mo.

Burton, Arista, '77, taught seventeen years. Colorado Sprimgs, Colo.

Caldwell, Beverly C., '76, taught twenty-three years. President State Normal, Natchitoches, La.

Caldwell, Delia, '78, taught seven years. Physician. Paducah, Ky.

Campbell, Harmon M., '87. Clerk. Chicago.

Cawthorn, Chris C., '84, taught six years. Crab Orchard.

Chandler, Larkin C.,'94, taught four years. Music teacher. Litchfield.

Cisne, W. G., '99. Cisne.

Clark, Lula, '91, taught seven years. East St. Louis.

Clements, Louis, '97, taught one year. Student Northwestern University. Chicago.

Clements, Robert, '98, taught one year. Student Northwestern University. Chicago.

Clendennen, Geo. E., '93, taught six years. Principal. Illiopolis.

Cochran, W. P., '92, taught three years. Editor. Marble Falls, Texas.

Cochran, Maud O., '94. Music teacher. Cape Girardeau, Mo.

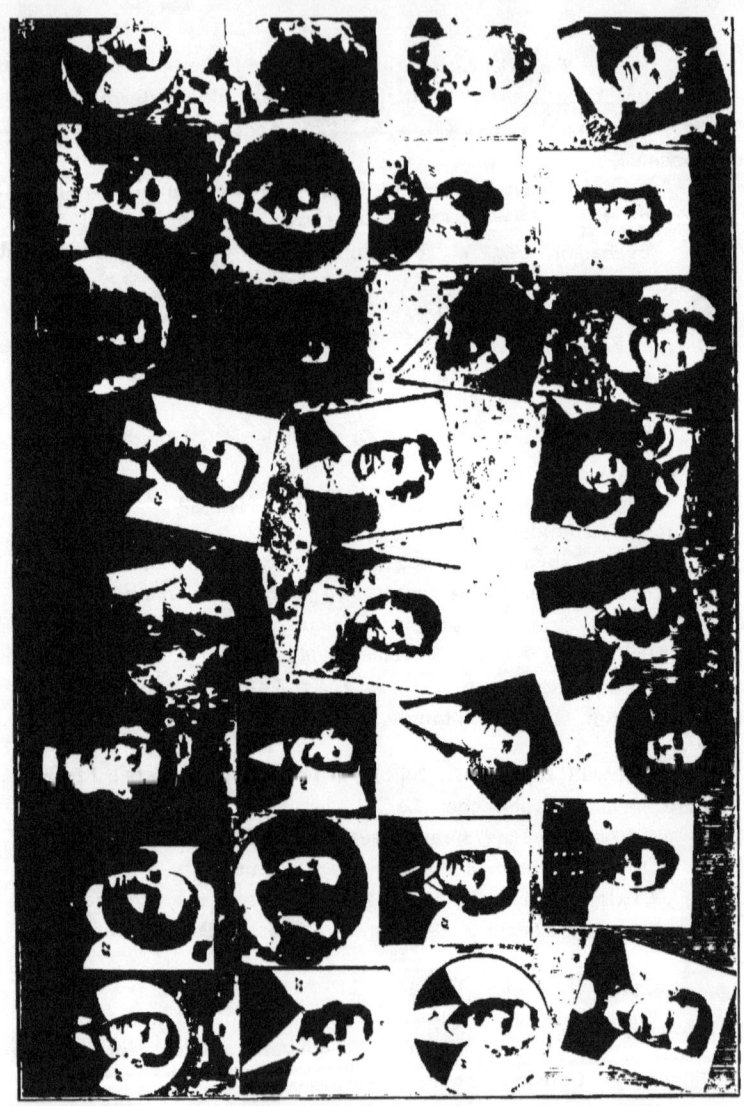

1. Margaret Anderson, '95.
2. Rhoda May Baker, '95.
3. Josie Barton Goodnow, '95.
4. Ola Baughman Bainum, '95.
5. Minnie Ferrell, '95.
6. Nora Ferrrell, '95.
7. David Oscar Jones, '95.
8. Albert Baker Kell, '95.
9. Homer Dalton Lee, '95.
10. Cora E. Nichols Jones, '95.
11. Emma H. Roane, '95.
12. Fred M. Snider, '95.
13. Charles J. Williams, '95.
14. Cincinnatus Boomer, '96.
15. Viola Cundiff Rendleman, '96
16. Guy E. Etherton, '96.
17. Minnie Ruth Flint, '96.
18. John P. Gilbert, '96.
19. Matilda Hobbs Snider, '96.
20. Ira O. Karraker, '96.
21. Leah C. McGahey, '96.
22. Richard H. Perrott, '96.
23. Samuel T. Robinson, '96.
24. Stella Royall Moore, '96.
25. Adelbert L. Spiller, '96.
26. Oscar T. Taylor, '96.
27. Bessie M. Thompson, '96.
28. Ralph Thompson, '96.
29. Laura M. Truscott, '96.
30. George D. Wham, '96.

**LIBRARY
OF THE
UNIVERSITY OF ILLINOIS**

Colyer, Frank H., '89, taught eight years. Professor in S. I. N. U. Carbondale.

Cortney, Alva C., '78, taught twenty-one years. Principal. Denver, Col.

Cowan, John F., '98, taught one year. Carterville,

Crane, Ezra, '96, taught two years. Railroad mail service. Tamaroa.

Crawford, Mary,'97, taught two years. Jonesboro.

Crawford, J. E., '99. Christopher.

Crawshaw, Solomon, '98. Carterville.

Curtis, Sarah L., '93, taught six years. Principal. Illiopolis.

Davidson, Mary (Mrs. J. T. Taylor, '95). Greenville.

Davis, Chas. H., '93, taught one year. Minister. Kampsville.

Dougherty, Andrew J., '94. Second Lieutenant regular army.

Duff, May B., '84, taught one year. Deceased.

Edman, Mate, '96, taught three years. Charleston.

Etherton, James M., '99. Carbondale.

Evans, Chas. E., '78. Deceased.

Farmer, Geo. H., '79, taught fourteen years. Vaundale, Ark.

Felts, William Troy, '94, taught five years. High school. Cairo.

Ferrell, Minnie, '95, taught four years. Carterville.

Ferrell, Nora, '95, taught one year. Carterville.

Fly, William C., '98, taught one year. Johnston City.

Freeman, James A., '91, taught eight years. Superintendent of schools. Trenton.

Fryar, Minnie J., '86. Librarian S. I. N. U. Carbondale.

Galbraith, Chas. M., '92. Physician. Carbondale.

Goodall, Samuel H., '87, taught two years. Lawyer. Marion.

Gray, Joseph, '80, taught fourteen years. Principal High School. Elgin.

Grove, Bessie L., '99. Carbondale.

Gilbert, Ida M., '98. Carbondale.

Glenn, William T., '93, taught five years. Belleville.

Goodall, Adella B. (Mrs. H. C. Mitchell), '82, taught three years. Carbondale.

Hackney, Kate G. (Mrs. F. O. Rogers), '90, taught three years. Waggoner.

Haldaman, Margaret, '99. Decatur.

Hall William H., '83, taught five years. Business manager of Lewis Institute. Chicago.

Haney, Thomas J., '95, taught three years. Principal. Atwood.

Hanna, James A., '78, taught six years. Merchant. Sulphur Springs, Ga.

Harker, Oliver A., '96. Student University of Illinois, Champaign.

Harmon, Mark D, '87, taught four years. Grayville, Ill.

Harris, W. O., '99. New Haven.

Hawkins, Cicero R., '87. State's Attorney. Pinckneyville, Ill.

Hawthorne, John C., '76.

Heitman, Louis, '80, taught four years. Pharmacist. Chester.

Hendee, Lu Bird, '84, taught seven years. Fairmount, Neb.

Henninger, Jennie, '93, taught five years. Student Chicago University.

Hewett, Emma L. (Mrs. W. H. Baltzer), taught three years. Hickman, Ky.

Hileman, Philetus E., '84. Lawyer. Jonesboro.

Hill, Mary A. (Mrs. E. L. Storment, '87), taught five years. Tempe, Ariz.

Hill, Mary E., '91, taught three years. Deceased.

Hillman, Orcelia B. (Mrs. Merrill, '78), taught five years. Saline, Kansas.

Hobbs, Matilda J. (Mrs. Fred Snider, '96), taught two years. Carbondale.

Hodge, Jennie (Mrs. W. T. Felts, '94), taught two years. Cairo.

Hooker, Lulu T., '99. Carbondale.

Holden, Emma (Mrs. H. A. Ross, '91), taught three years. St. Louis, Mo.

Hord, Kittie E. (Mrs. C. M. Morgan, '86), taught ten years. Portland, Oregon.

Hubbard, Mary E. (Mrs. Frank Watson, '93), taught five years. Greenville.

Hubbard, Samuel A., '93, taught two years. Lawyer. Mount Sterling.

Hull, Chas. E., '80. Member State Senate. Salem.

Hull, Gertrude, '85, taught four years. Latin teacher, High School, Milwaukee, Wis.

Hull, Bertha, '90, taught four years. Assistant in Drawing. Ipsilanti, Mich.

Hundley, Louella.

Hypes, Cornelia A., '98, taught one year. Carbondale.

Jack, Jessie, '98, taught one year. Kinmundy.

Jay, Norman A., '94, taught four years. Steeleville.

Jenkins, John H., '84, taught thirteen years. Superintendent of schools. Cobden.

Johnson, Calla, '88, taught one year. Carbondale.

Johnston, Lewis E., '87, taught one year. Lawyer. Keysport.

Karraker, Orville M,, '99, Dongola.

Kell, Omer Adrian, '93. Physician. Salem.

Kell, Albert Baker, '95, taught one year. Carter.

Kellar, Kent E., 90, taught three years. Lawyer. Ava.

Kennedy, George R., '78, taught one year. Merchant. Murphysboro.

Kennedy, Maggie, '86, taught four years. Mexico City, Mex.

Kimmell, Henry A., '80, taught six years. Farmer. Calhoun.

Kimmell, E. Lee, '92, taught seven years. Carmi.

Kimmell, Ruby I., '92, taught seven years. East St. Louis.

Kimzy, Walter R., '89, taught nine years. County Superintendent. Tamaroa.

Krysher, Alice (Mrs. W. H. Livingston, '82), taught four years. Pana.

Lacy, Rurie O., '85, taught one year. Physician. Lake City, Col.

Lakin, Edwin F., '94, taught three years. Rochester.

Lancaster, Tilman A., '85, taught three years. Lawyer. Lexington, Tenn.

Lawrence, Bertha, '87, taught eleven years. Tipton, Ia.

Lawrence, J. H. '91, taught six years. Professor Park College, Parksville, Mo.

Lawrence, Blanche, '92, taught six years. Chicago.

Lee, Homer Dalton, '95, taught three years. Merchant. Carbondale.

Lightfoot, Richard T., '84, taught two years. Lawyer. Paducah, Kentucky.

Lirely, William H., '92, taught two years. Signal Service. Indianapolis, Ind.

Longbons, Edward, '94, taught five years. Superintendent, Metropolis.

Loomis, Carrie I., '86, taught one year. Thompsonville.

Loomis, Lydia M., '91, taught four years. Belvidere.

Mann, Wallace., '80, taught four years. Editor. Decatur.

Marberry, William T., '97, taught two years. Belknap.
Marchildon, John W., '99. Thebes.
Martin, John, '83, taught four years. Physician. Tolono.
McAnally, John T., '78, taught three years. Physician. Carbondale.
McAnally, Mary (Mrs. N. H. Moss), '78, taught ten years. Mt. Vernon.
McAnally, Fannie D. (Mrs. D. B. Fager), '86, taught one year. Salem.
McAnally, Jessie F., '97, taught two years. Mt. Vernon.
McConaghie, Thomas, '99. Oakdale.
McCormick, George, '96. Farmington.
McCreery, Ida M., '79, taught three years. Deceased.
McKittrick, F. D., '99. Fairfield.
Mc Kown, James Edgar, '97, taught two years. Paxton.
McMackin, Edward G., '87, taught two years. Dentist. Salem.
Miller, John E., '85, taught twelve years. East St. Louis.
Mohlenbrock, Eric, '94, taught one year. Deceased.
Moore, Jack N., '93, taught five years. Principal. Walnut Ridge, Ark.
Morgan, Chas. M., '88, taught one year. Bradstreets Agency. Portland, Ore.
Morton, Ralph B., '92, taught two years. Lawyer. Carterville.
Munger, Robert P., '98. Clerk. Carbondale.
Murphy, W. Gordon, '99. Carbondale.
Nave, Della A. (Mrs. P. E. Hileman, '83), taught four years. Jonesboro.
Nichols, John B., '92, taught six years. California.
Ogle, Albert B., '80. Insurance Agent. Belleville.
Ozment, Fannie, '98, taught one year. Decatur.
Palmer, Myrtle I., '99. Custer Park.
Parkinson, Arthur E., '82. Associate Editor National Cyclopedia American Biographies. Chicago.
Parkinson, J. M., '89, taught nine years. City Superintendent Schools, Edwardsville.
Parkinson, Daniel M., '97. Manager Telephone Exchange, Carbondale.
Parkinson, Franklin A., '98. Assistant Clerk. Murphysboro.
Parks, Elizabeth, '89, taught seven years. Training Teacher S. I. N. U. Carbondale.

1. Bertram Amon, '97.
2. R. Jane Barter, '97.
3. Mary Crawford, '97.
4. Arthur G. Cross, '97.
5. William A. Etherton, '97.
6. May K. Hayes, '97.
7. Jay T. Kirk, '97.
8. Uriah Kissinger, '97.
9. William T. Marberry, '97.
10. Nellie Weller, '97.
11. Harry J. Alvis, '98.
12. James W. Barrow, '98.
13. Andrew S. Boucher, '98.
14. Nina O. Buchanan, '93.
15. Solomon Crawshaw, '98.
16. William C. Fly, '98.
17. Margaret Huggins, '98.
18. Fannie Ozment, '98.
19. Frank A. Parkinson, '98.
20. Lucy H. Patten, '98.
21. C. A. Quackenbush, '98.
22. Andrew E. Shepherd, '98.
23. Kate Snider, '98.
24. Edna Thornton, '98.
25. Nina Thornton, '98.
26. William L. Toler, '98.
27. Margaret Wilson, '98.

**LIBRARY
OF THE
UNIVERSITY OF ILLINOIS**

Patten, Arthur E., '92. Salesman. Chicago.
Patten, Lucy H., '98, taught one year, Pomona.
Patterson, John E., '95, taught four years. High School. Evansville, Ind.
Perry, Mary Helen, '98, taught one year. Decatur.
Peters, Mabel K., '96, taught two years. Carbondale.
Peters, Helen N., '97. Student Washington University. St. Louis.
Phillips, Lyman T., '79, taught two years. Dentist. Nashville.
Phillips, Myrtle K. (Mrs. H. Z. Zuck), '94. Tempe, Ariz.
Pickrell, Per, '97, taught two years. El Paso.
Pierce, Reuben E., '78, taught one year. Minister. Epworth.
Plant, Richmond, '78. St. Louis, Mo.
Pruett, Chas. F., '99. Kinmundy.
Pugh, Chas. H., '94, taught five years. Colorado.
Quackenbush, Chas. A., '98, taught one year. McClure.
Ragsdale, Joseph S., '92, taught six years. Superintendent. North Judson, Ind.
Ramsey, Joseph Eli, '90, taught nine years. County Superintendent. Mount Carmel.
Reef, Edmund W., '97. Postal Clerk. Carbondale.
Renfro, Robert E., '93. Real Estate and Loan Agent. Carbondale.
Rentchler, Frank P., '80. Los Angeles, Cal.
Rhoads, Miriam E. '98, taught one year. Metropolis.
Ridenhower, Carrie (Mrs. J. L. Mount, '84), taught four years. Deceased.
Richards, Kate E. (Mrs. W. A. Stewart, '88), taught two years. Deceased.
Robarts, Mary A. (Mrs. M. H. Ogden, '85), taught eight years. Carbondale.
Roberts, George L., '96. Corinth.
Roberts, Arthur, '97, taught one year. Superintendent. Golconda.
Robinson, Edward H., '78. Physician. Chicago.
Roe, Nellie Bell, '97, taught one year. Carbondale.
Roe, Edith, '99. Carbondale.
Royal, Stella Ethel (Mrs. Moore), '96, taught one year, Villa Ridge.
Rude, Otto J., '93, taught six years. Superintendent. Carbondale.
Sams, Fountain F., '90, taught one year. Lawyer. East St. Louis.

Searing, Harry R., '87. City Treasurer. Carbondale.

Scott, Luther T., '87, taught one year. Editor. Carbondale.

Sheppard, Lizzie M. (Mrs. Dr. J. K. Miller), '80, taught eight and one-half years. Greeley, Colo.

Smith, Seva A. (Mrs. G. S. Hoag), '87. Denver, Colo.

Smith, Mabel, '90. Deceased.

Smith, Edgar A., '94. Medical Student. Chicago.

Snider, Lydia E., '87, taught ten years. North Evanston.

Snider, Fred M., '95. Merchant. Carbondale.

Snider, Kate, '98. Carbondale.

Sowell, Myrtle I., '95, taught two years. Paducah, Ky.

Sowers, Mary A. (Mrs. J. C. Scott), '81, taught eight years. Carbondale.

Sprecher, Edgar L., '83, taught five years. Merchant. Guatemala, C. A.

Sprecher, Theo. M., '91, taught five years. Crittenden, Ariz.

Steele, Robert E., '91, taught one year. Physician. Lehi, Utah.

Stern, Lewis, '91, taught eight years. Superintendent. Fountain City, Wis.

Stewart, Henry A., '82. Physician. Chicago.

Stewart, Ellen, '97, taught two years. Elko.

Stewart, Josephine, '99. Carbondale.

Storment, Edgar L., '86, taught eleven years. Deceased.

Storment, John C., '90, taught nine years. Principal. Pamona, California.

Stout, Chas. L., '93, taught one year. Deceased.

Street, Jasper N., '88, taught eleven years. Superintendent City Schools, Vandalia.

Taylor, Oscar T., '96. Traveling Salesman. St. Louis.

Thomas, Maud, '84. Deceased.

Thomas, Kate (Mrs. D. L. Chapman, '85), taught four years. Murphysboro.

Thompson, Ralph, '96. Student University Illinois, Champaign.

Thompson, Bessie M., '96. Carbondale.

Torrance, Anna Eliza, '90, taught seven years. Salem.

Treat, Chas. W., '84. Prof. Natural Science, Lawrence University. Appleton, Wis.

Trobaugh, Frank E., '88, taught one year. Deceased.

Turner, George T., '87, taught two years. County Judge. Vandalia.

Warder, William H., '76, taught three years. Member of General Assembly. Marion.

Warder, Gertrude A. (Mrs. C. J. Mitchlet), '80, taught eight years. Willmette.

Wobkemeyer, Chas. W., '99. Campbell Hill.

White, Maude, '97, taught two years. Carbondale.

Whitney, William, '91, taught two years. Railroad Mail Service. Carbondale.

Whittenburg, Sarah J., '93, taught eight years. County Superintendent. Vienna.

Williams, Cora (Mrs. R. W. Wiley), '86, taught two years. Pomona, Cal.

Williams, Chas. J., '95. Clerk. Carbondale.

Woods, John W., '82, taught fifteen years. Principal. Floresville, Texas.

Woods, William H., '97, taught two years. Lockhart, Texas.

Woodson, Myrtle F., '93, taught five years. Austin.

Wright, Mary, '76, taught two and one-half years. Cobden.

Yourex, Mable Clare, '65, taught four years. Principal. Calumet, Mich.

~The Most Notable American Texts

and the texts which are as attractive for home reading or for gifts as they are for profitable school work, are published by the

American Book Company

They represent *School-Book Making as a High Art;* not high art in form and illustration alone, but also in the richness of their material, their advanced principles of education, their practical methods, and the skill by which the knowledge that they contain is adapted to the needs of everyday school requirements. These texts embrace almost all branches of knowledge, and provide for the progress and mental development of learners from the kindergarten to the college. In their perfect fitness to the needs of pupils and their agreement with all the best in educational theory and practice, they are justly entitled to their recognized position as

The Leading American Texts.

For descriptions, price-lists and catalogues of these books please write to the

AMERICAN BOOK COMPANY

New York   Cincinnati   Chicago   Boston
         Atlanta, Ga.   Portland, Ore.

→1898-1899.←

University of Illinois

Fifteen Buildings. 214 Instructors. 375 Courses of Instruction. Summer Term, 1899, June 19th—August 18th. . . . . .

ATTENDANCE, '90-'91, 519; '91-'92, 583; '92-'93, 714; '93-'94, 743; '94-'95, 810; '95-'96, 855; '96-'97, 1076; '97-'98, 1585; '98-'99, 1824.

COLLEGES, Literature and Arts, Agriculture, Science, Engineering.

SCHOOLS, Music, Art and Design, Military Science.
State Library School. (Only one in the West).
School of Law. (Exclusive time of Instructors).
School of Medicine—College of Physicians and Surgeons, Chicago.
School of Pharmacy—Chicago College of Pharmacy, Chicago.
GRADUATE SCHOOL.

LITERATURE AND LANGUAGE, Work has strongly advanced.

ARCHITECTURE, Department without a rival in the West.

EDUCATION, (Science of), Advanced work unsurpassed.

ENGINEERING, The equipment in Civil, Electrical, Mechanical, Sanitary and Railroad Egineering is of the best.
New Astronomical Observatory.

SCIENCES, Liberally provided for. State Laboratory of Natural History. United States Agriculture Experiment Station. University Biological Experiment Station on Illinois river.

WOMAN'S DEPARTMENT, Two hundred students.

Library of 50,000 volumes. Military band, orchestra, oratorio society, glee club, ladies' glee club, male quartet, mandolin and guitar club, etc. Much attention paid to athletics. Laboratories mechanical shops, experimental farms, literary societies, Young Men's and Young Women's Christian Associations.

TUITION FREE IN ACADEMIC COURSES.

The University of Illinois has attained first rank. Graduates will certainly lose no opportunity to add to its strength. Remember it with a gift. Send children and friends to it; it can do all that any and much more than most institutions can do for them. It will supply the most thorough instruction in any study. Write for information. When practicable come and see and appreciate the advances which have been made.

For catalogues, circulars, or specific information, address
W. L. PILLSBURY, Registrar,
At either Champaign or Urbana, Ill.

Cyr's Readers.

The helpful and elevating influence of good literature upon young minds has long been recognized by progressive teachers. To find a series of readers that will at once interest the pupil confronts the careful and conscientious teacher. Cyr's Readers exactly meet this need. They are based upon a definite literary plan which has been consistently carried out. The outline given below will show how the author has introduced the child to the great American and English writers.

Primer, 106 pages 24
First Reader, 111 pages 28
Second Reader (based upon the works of Longfellow, & Whittier) *197 p.* 36
Third Reader (based upon the works of Lowell, Holmes, Bryant) *280 p.* 50
Fourth Reader (Irving, Scott, Dickens, Hawthorne, Tennyson,) *380 p.* 60
Fifth Reader (Prescott, Cooper, Wordsworth, Milton, Motley, Goldsmith, Shakespeare, Burns,)
Ready July 1.

◆◆◆◆◆◆◆

Speer's Arithmetics.

Recognize sense-training as the basis of thought, and definite relations of magnitude as the only basis of mathematical inferences. They advance the study from the science of number to that of definite relations of quantity. They make simple ratios the key to the solution of all problems. They unfold the pupil's mind, not only by leading him to perceive, but also to form judgments and to reason. In short, they are wholly sensible and pedagogical.

A Primary Arithmetic (for teachers,) *154 p.* 35
Elementary Arithmetic (for pupils,) *314 p.* 45
An Advanced Arithmetic ...... (for grammar grades,)
In Preparation.

◆◆◆◆◆◆◆

Correspondence invited.

GINN & COMPANY, Publishers,
BOSTON.   NEW YORK.   CHICAGO.   LONDON.
Chicago Office 378-388 Wabash Avenue.

H. C. MITCHELL, PRESIDENT. F. T. JOYNER, CASHIER. W. W. CLEMENS, VICE-PRESIDENT.

Organized Under Laws of Illinois.

Jackson State Bank,

CARBONDALE, ILL.

Paid-up Capital $25,000.

Does a general banking business. Special attention given to collections. Lafety Deposit Boxes on reasonable terms.

School Apparatus and Supplies.

Globes, Maps, Charts, Blackboards and Blackboard Material of every description. Physical and Chemical Apparatus. Diplomas and School Stationery.

Science Tablets, for laboratory notes and drawings in physiography, biology, physics and chemistry. Manufacturers of Bock-Steger Automatic Models and Politico Relief Maps.

We are headquarters for everything required in the school-room. Give us an opportunity to make prices on such supplies as you need.

Central School Supply House,

WABASH AND RANDOLPH STS., CHICAGO, ILL.

E. PATTEN & SON,

Prescription Druggists.

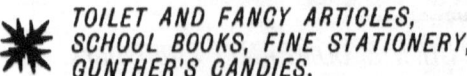
TOILET AND FANCY ARTICLES,
SCHOOL BOOKS, FINE STATIONERY,
GUNTHER'S CANDIES.

West Side Square.   **Carbondale, Ill.**

BUY GOODS IN CHICAGO

Have you tried the Catalogue system of buying EVERYTHING you use at Wholesale Prices? We can save you 15 to 40 per cent. on your purchases. We are now erecting and will own and occupy the highest building in America, employ 2,000 clerks filling country orders exclusively, and will refund purchase price if goods don't suit you.

Our General Catalogue—1,000 pages, 16,000 illustrations, 60,000 quotations—costs us 72 cents to print and mail. We will send it to you upon receipt of 15 cents, to show your good faith.

MONTGOMERY WARD & CO.
MICHIGAN AVE. AND MADISON ST.
CHICAGO.

F. A. PRICKETT,   WM. A. SCHWARTZ,   E. E. MITCHELL,
PRESIDENT.   VICE-PRESIDENT,   CASHIER.

First National Bank,
Carbondale, Ill.

D. R. Harrison,
(Herrins Prairie, Ill.)
O. A. Harker,
E. E. Mitchell,
J. C. Hundley,
J. M. Dillinger,
J. D. Peters,
N. J. Powers,
   (Makanda, Ill.)
F. A. Prickett,
Wm. A. Schwartz.

Capital, $50,000.
Surplus and Profit, $12,500.

Transacts a general banking business. Every commodation consistent with sound banking methods extended to our customers.

Opera House Building.   East Side Square.

Magazine and Library Binding.

IT IS A GREAT MISTAKE not to bind your Magazines and periodicals containing, as they do, the most advanced thought in all departments of literature by authorities of unlimited resources.

At Small Expense

For binding such publications will make a valuable addition to your library not comprehended by other books. Send for illustrated price list, stating what you have and quantity.

Librarians Should Not Fail

To get our estimates for rebinding miscellaneous and reference books, as well as periodical publications.

Ward Brothers, Jacksonville, Ill.

W. E. CLINGENPEEL,
Jeweler, Watchmaker
AND OPTICIAN.

West Side.   **Carbondale, Ill.**

www.ingramcontent.com/pod-product-compliance
Lightning Source LLC
Chambersburg PA
CBHW020803230426
43666CB00007B/837